Gramma Bella's Family

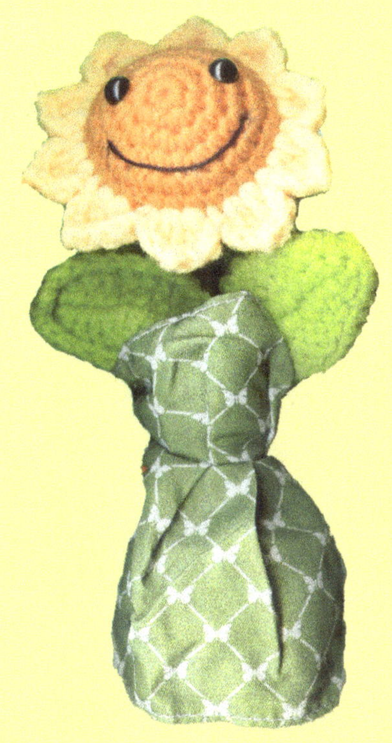

Barbara Swift Guidotti

NatureScan Books
Fort Myers, Florida

Book and cover design by NatureScan Books

www.naturescanart.com.

ISBN: 979-8-3303-8239-2

Summary: Gramma Bella creates a large family by adopting those who are lost and alone.

ART000000 Art / General
SEL021000 Self-Help / Motivational & Inspirational
FAM004000 Family / Adoption & Fostering

Published and Printed in the United States of America
First Edition

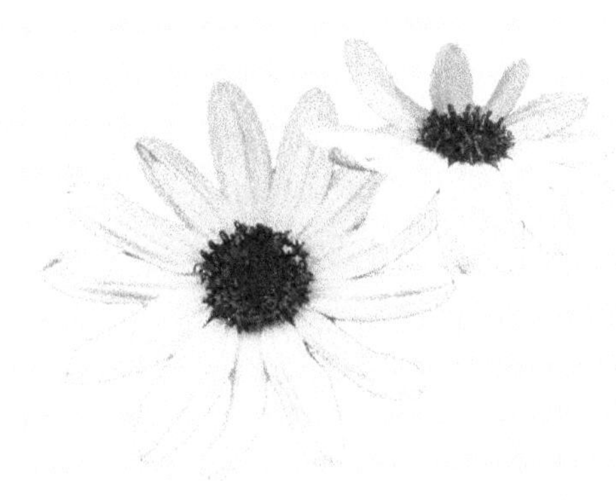

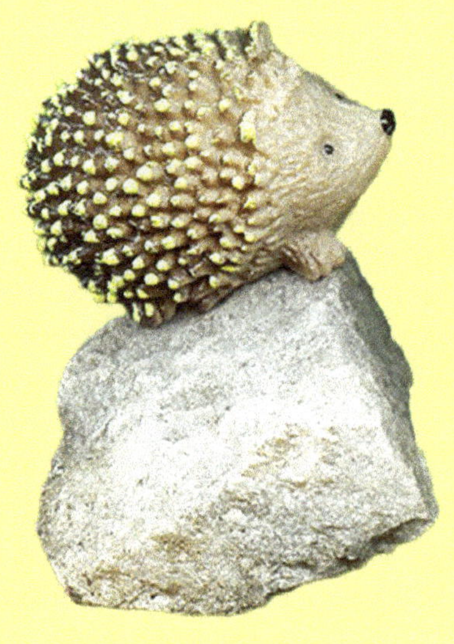

To all who for one reason or
another know how it feels to be
lonely and alone..

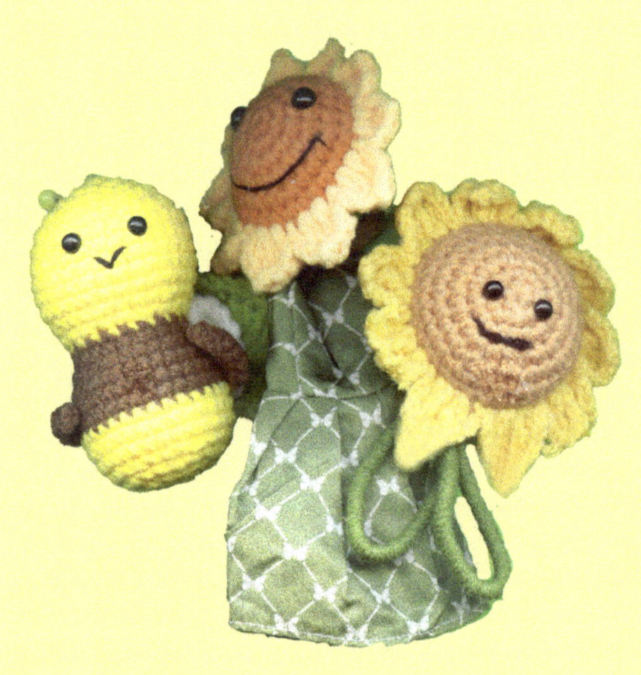

*Little souls find their way to you whether they're
from your womb or someone else's.*

—Sheryl Crow

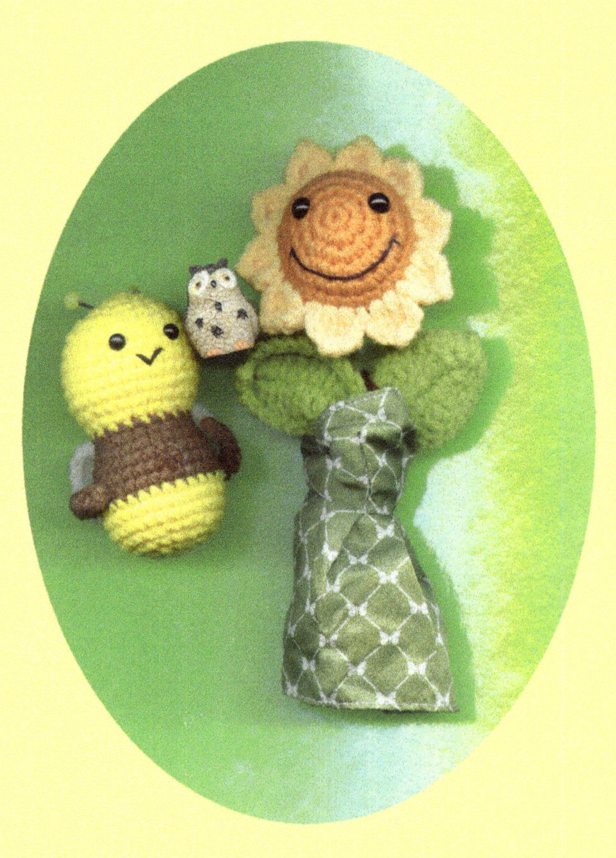

Gramma Bella's Family

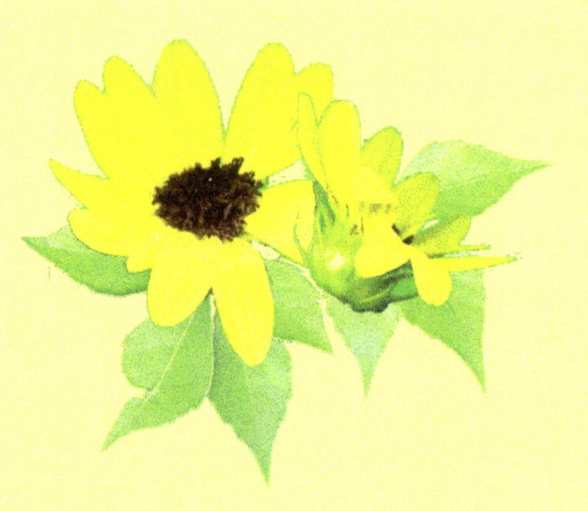

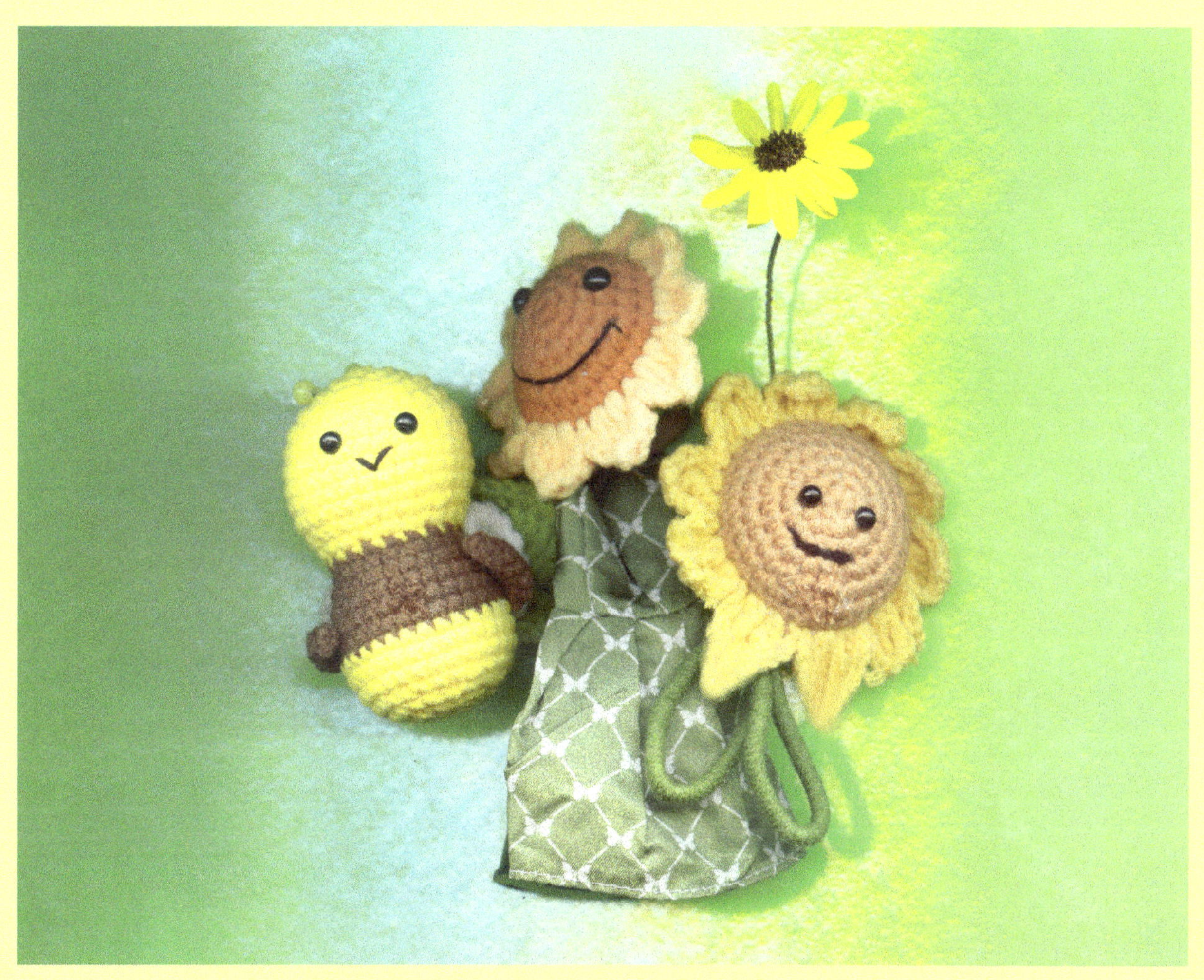

Buzz and Ginger were found and adopted by
Gramma Bella.

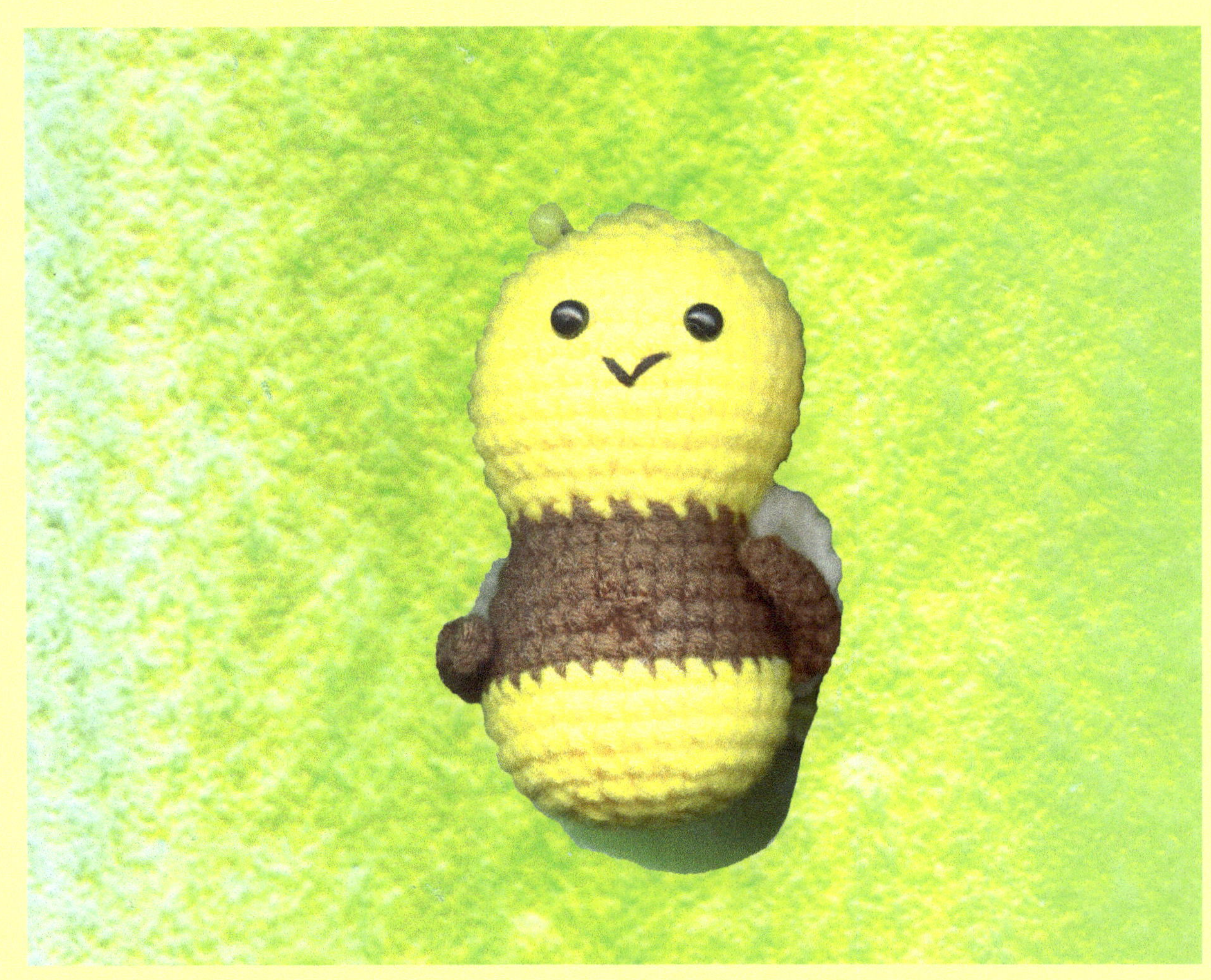

Buzz's mother was a Queen Bee who had
been killed by pesticides.

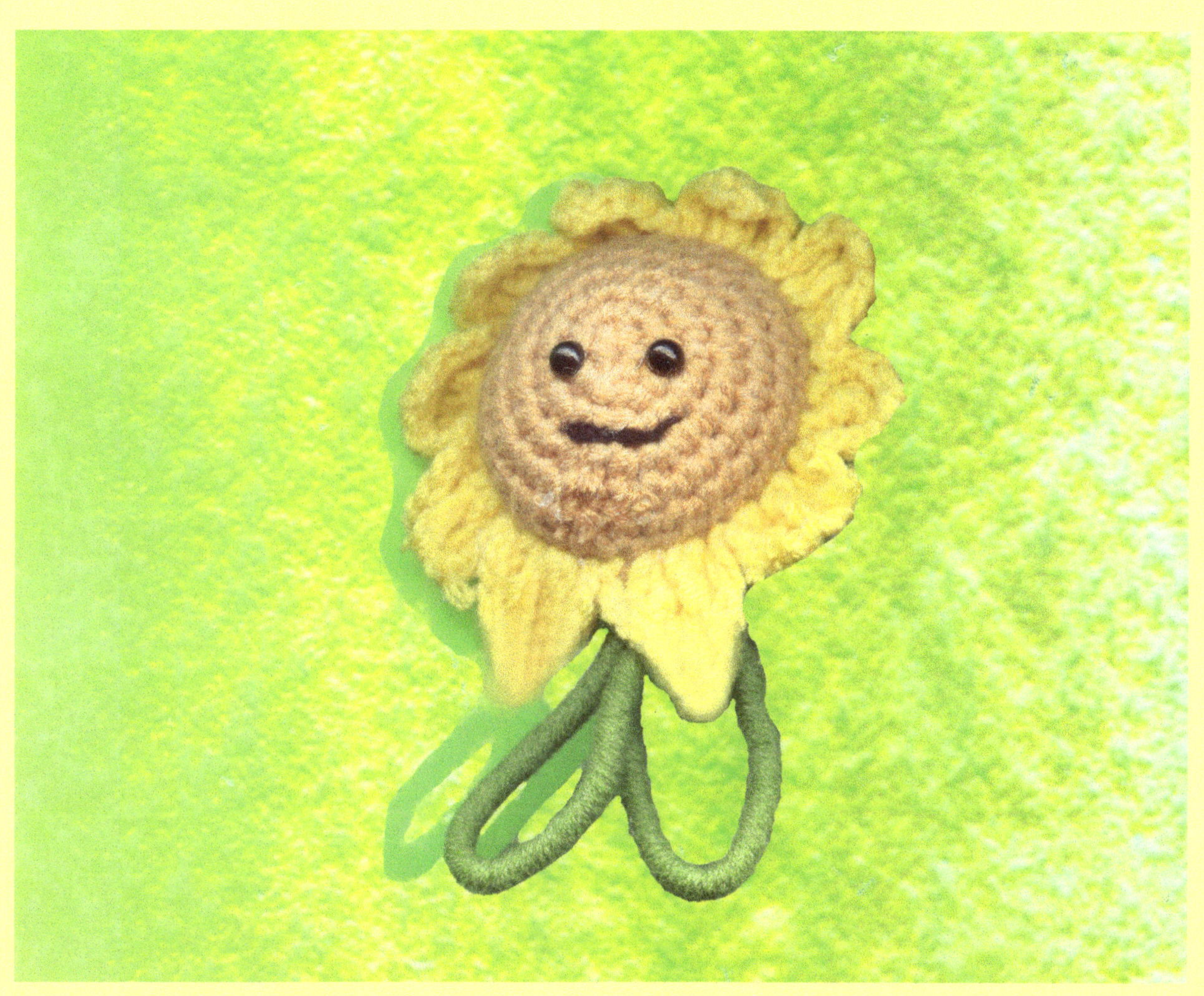

Ginger had lost her family in a hurricane.

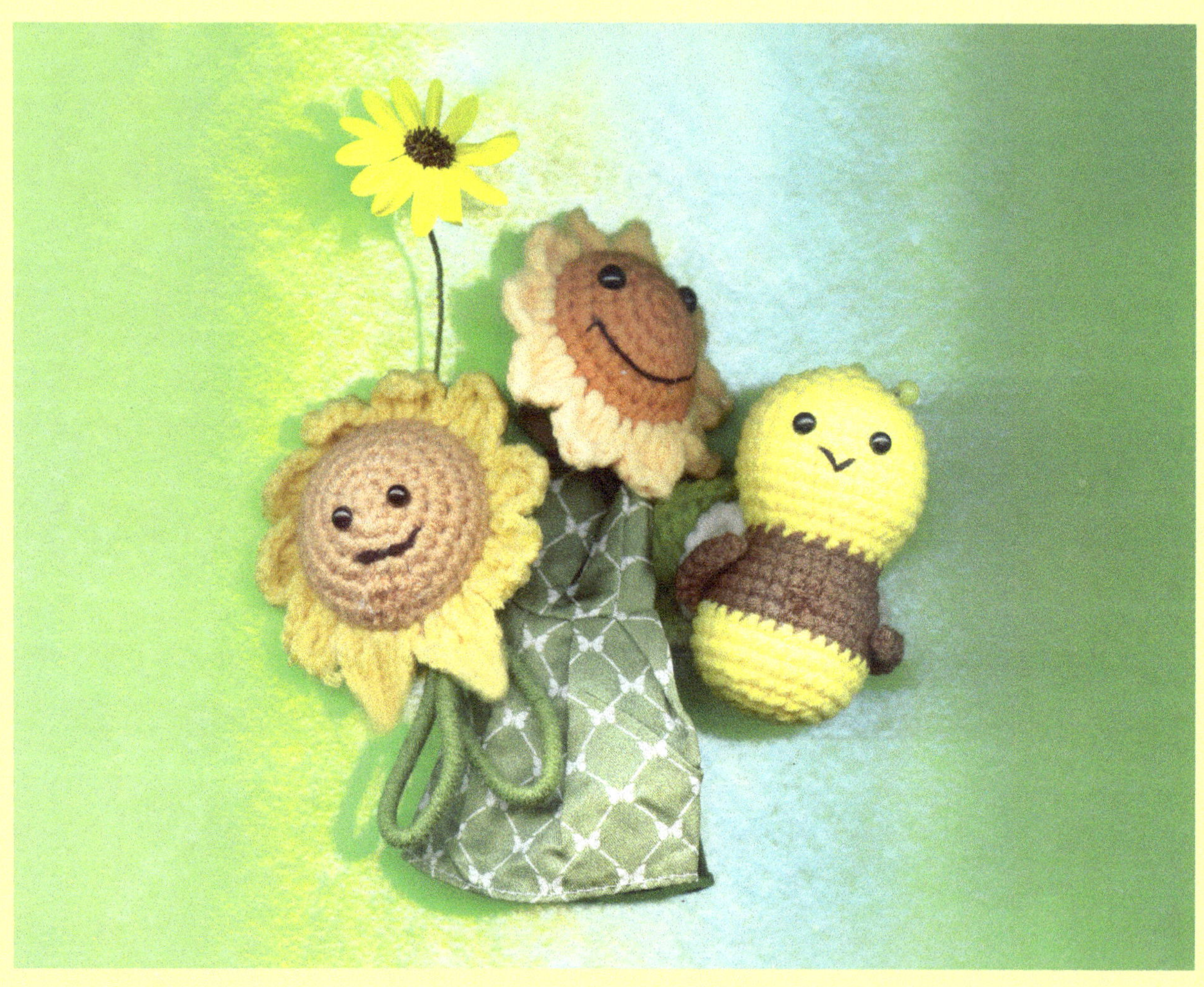

In the spirit of Gramma Bella, Buzz and Ginger
went out to find others who were alone and lonely.

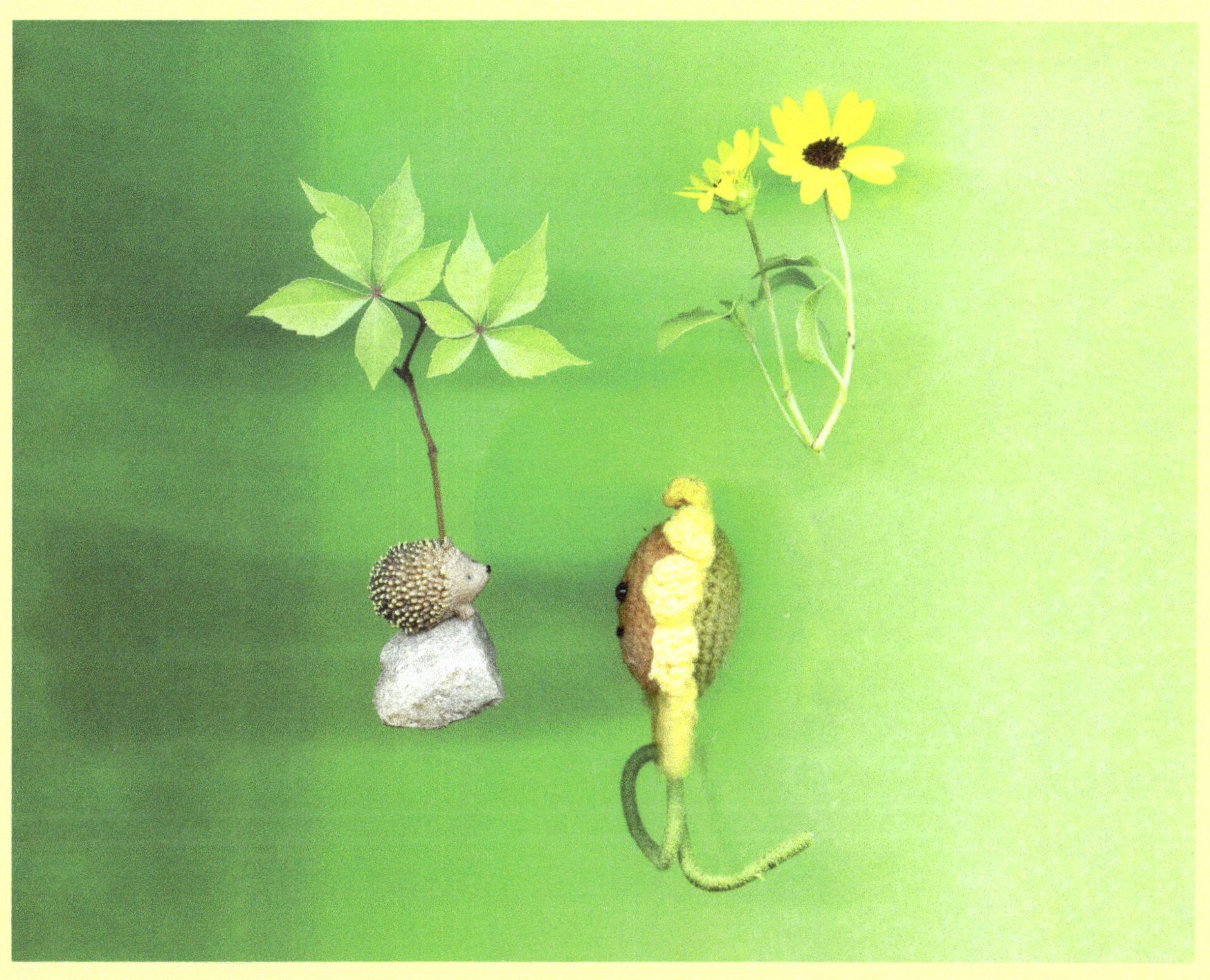

Ginger found Harriet the Hedgehog at the edge
of the woods.

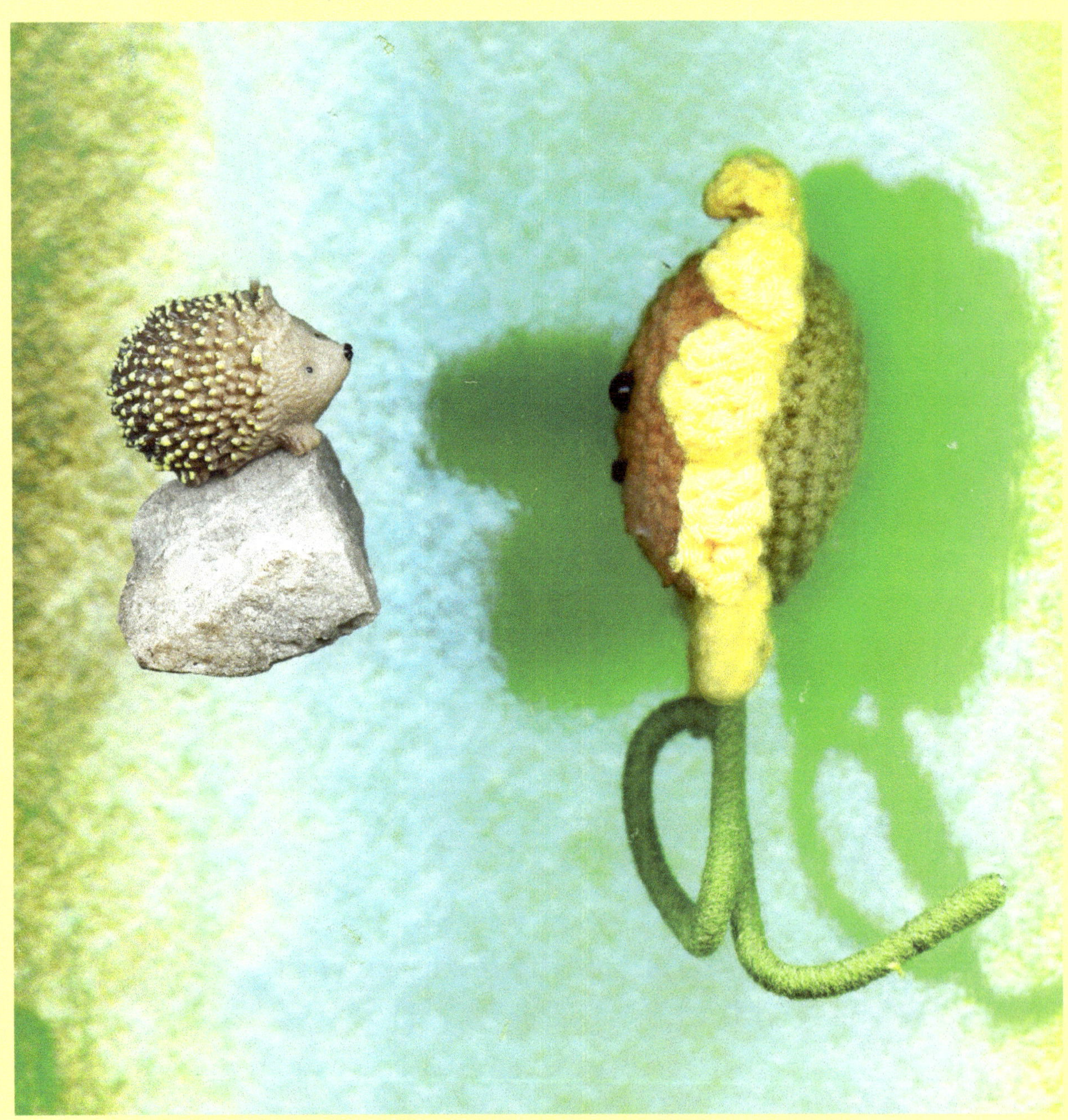

Harriet was very sad.

She told Ginger that she had wandered onto a boat that had carried her far away from her family in England.

Now she was all alone.

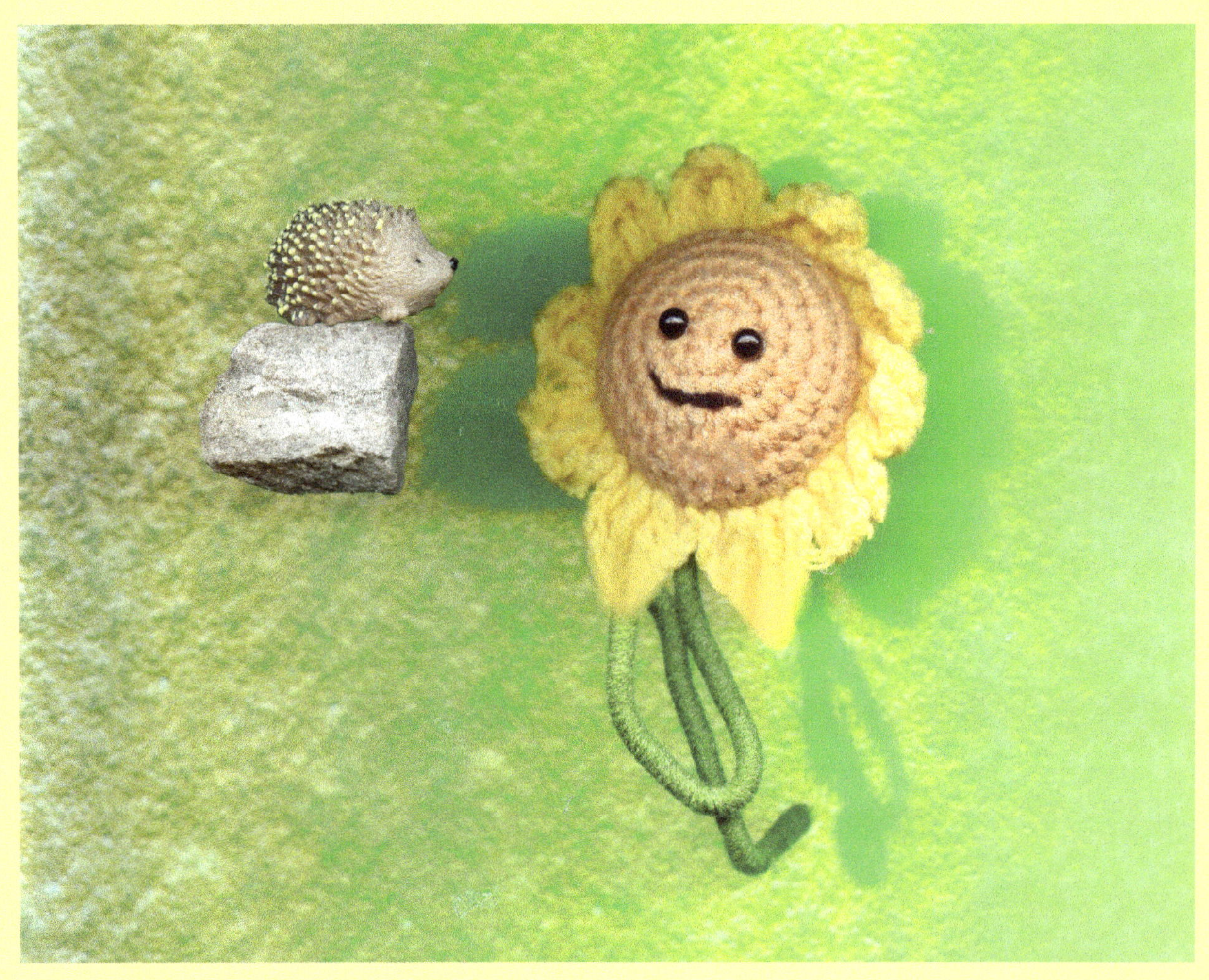

"Not anymore!" said Ginger.

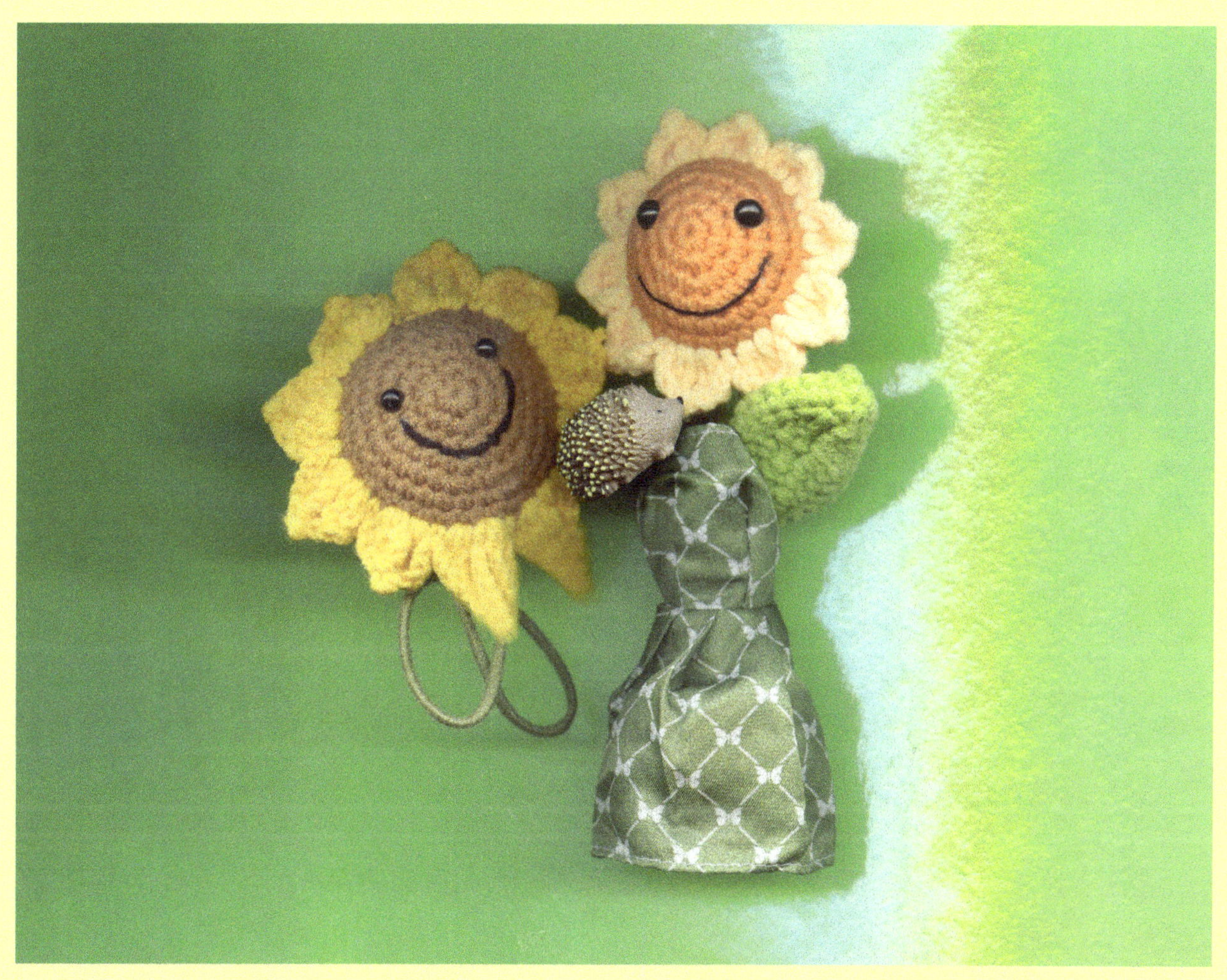

Ginger took Harriet with her to Gramma Bella.

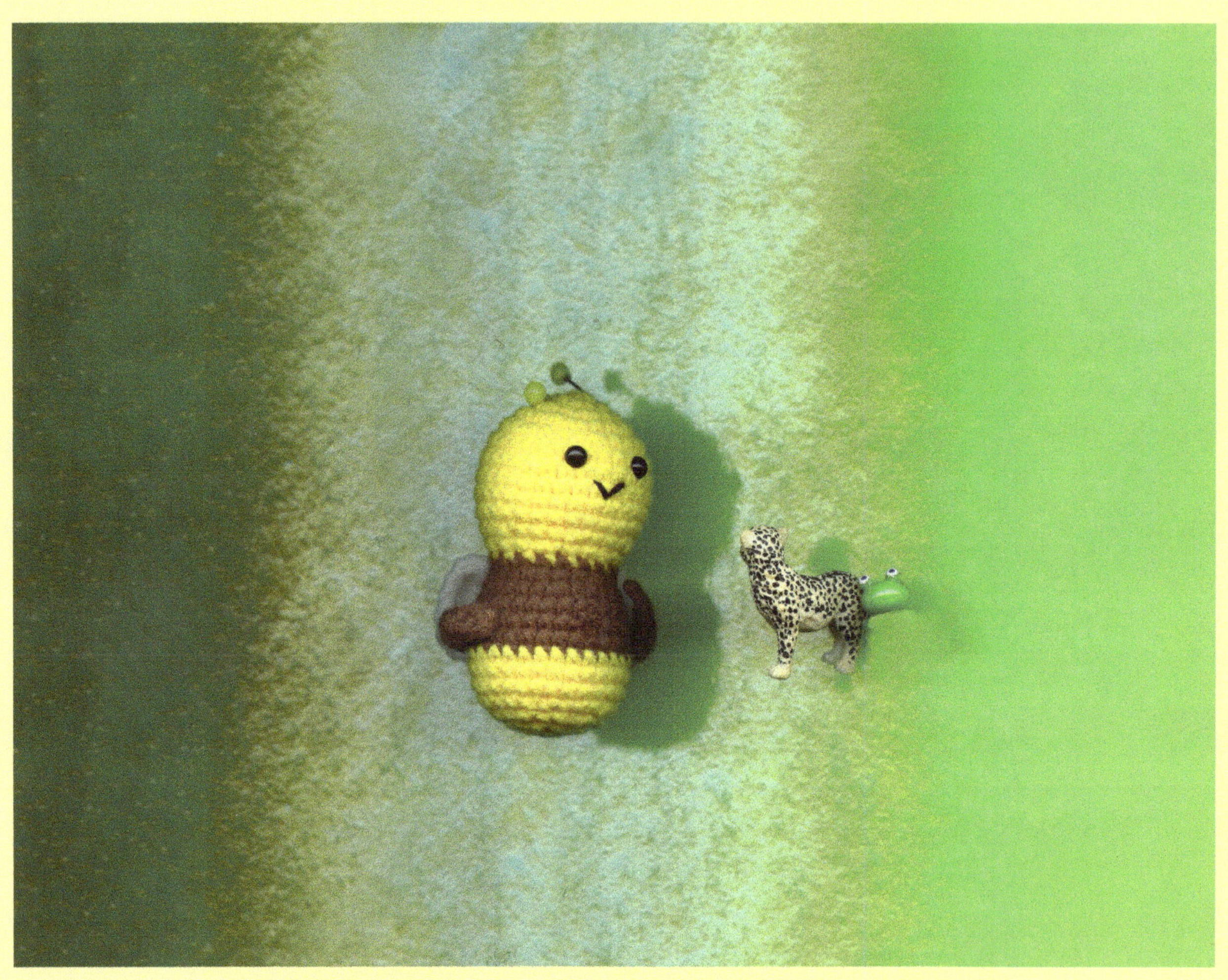

Buzz found Charley, a baby cheetah with only
three legs.
He had a pet frog.

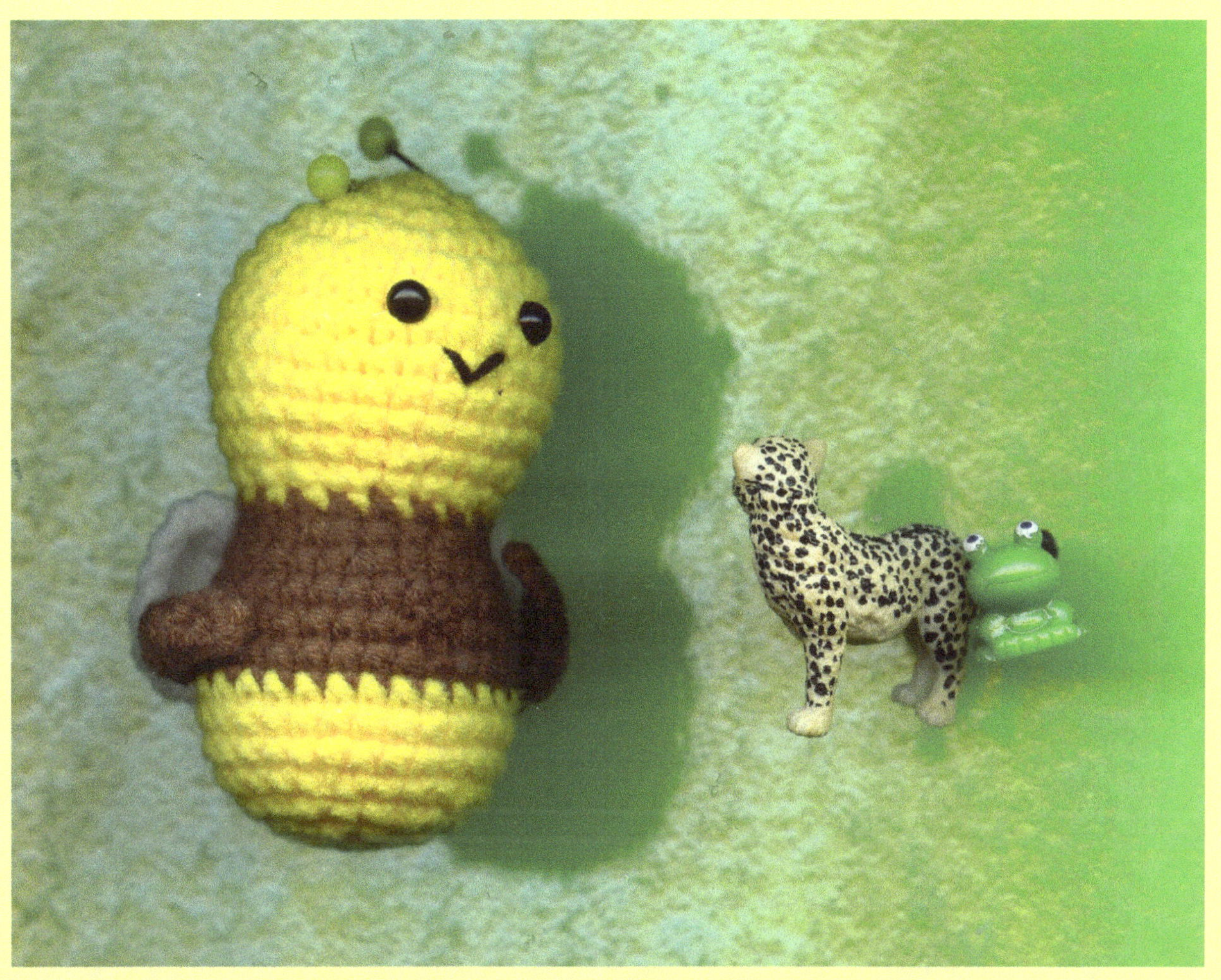

Charley told Buzz that he couldn't keep up with his brothers and sisters after he had lost one of his legs.

Now he was all alone.

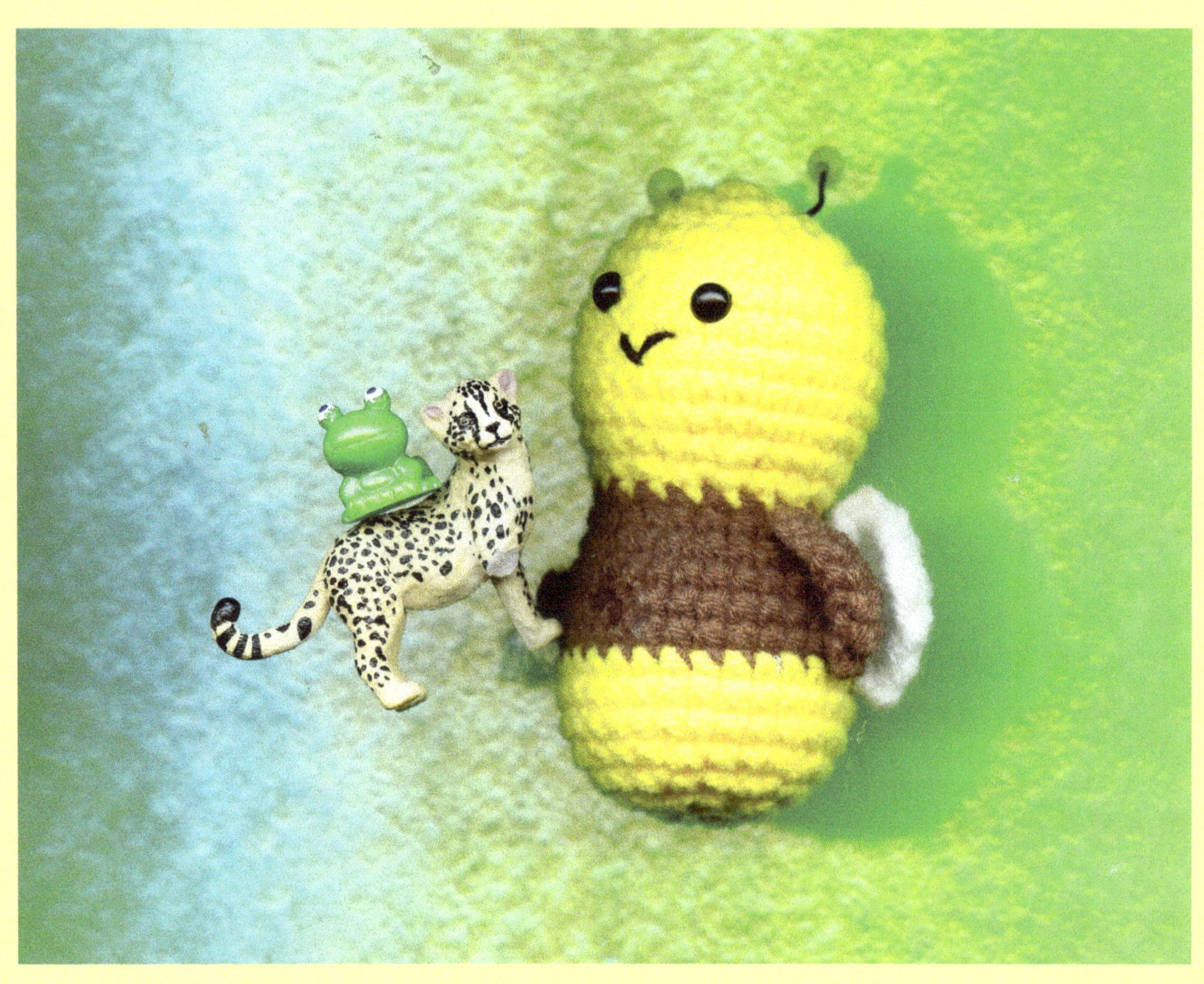

"Not anymore!" said Buzz.

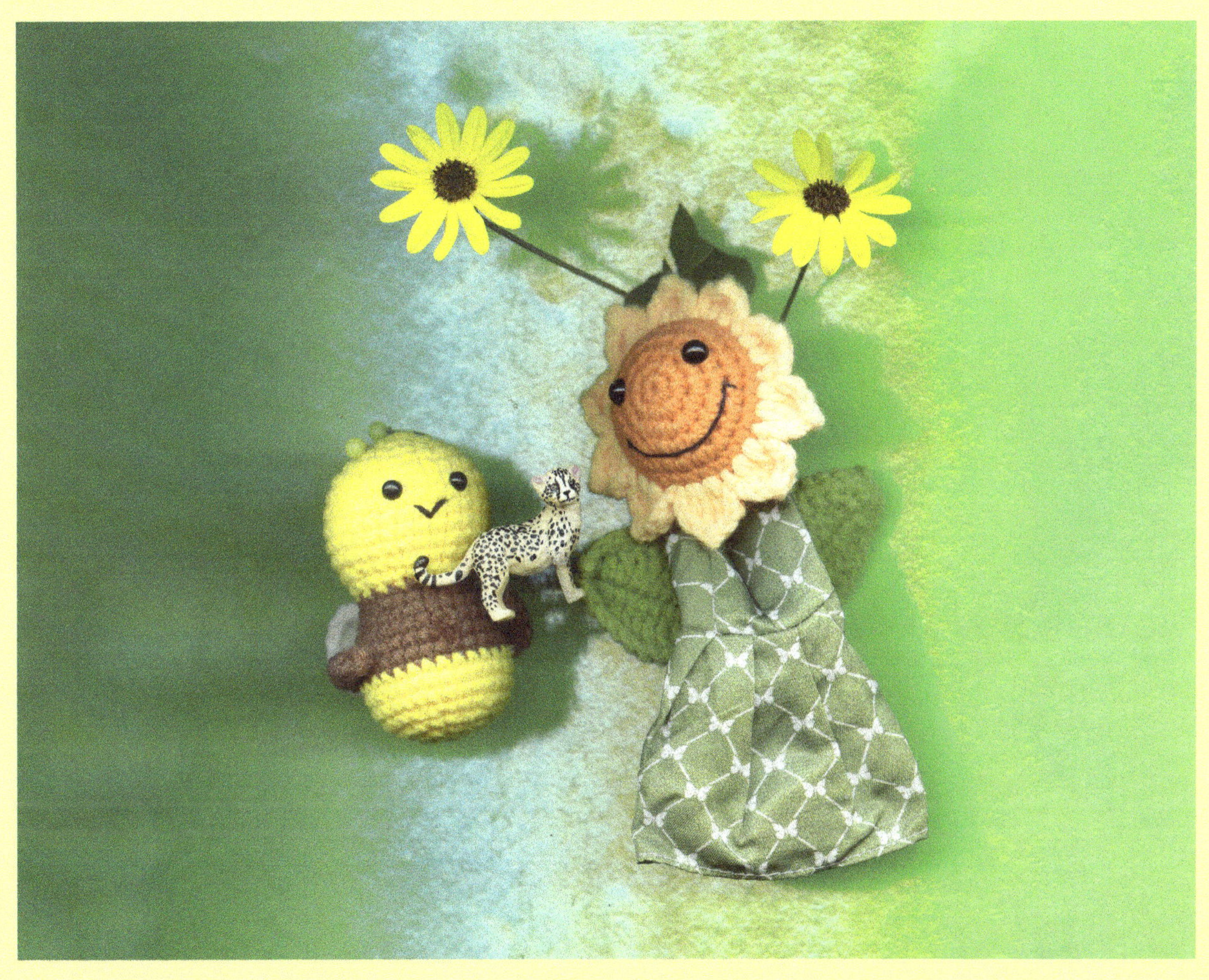

Buzz took Charley and his pet frog to
Gramma Bella.

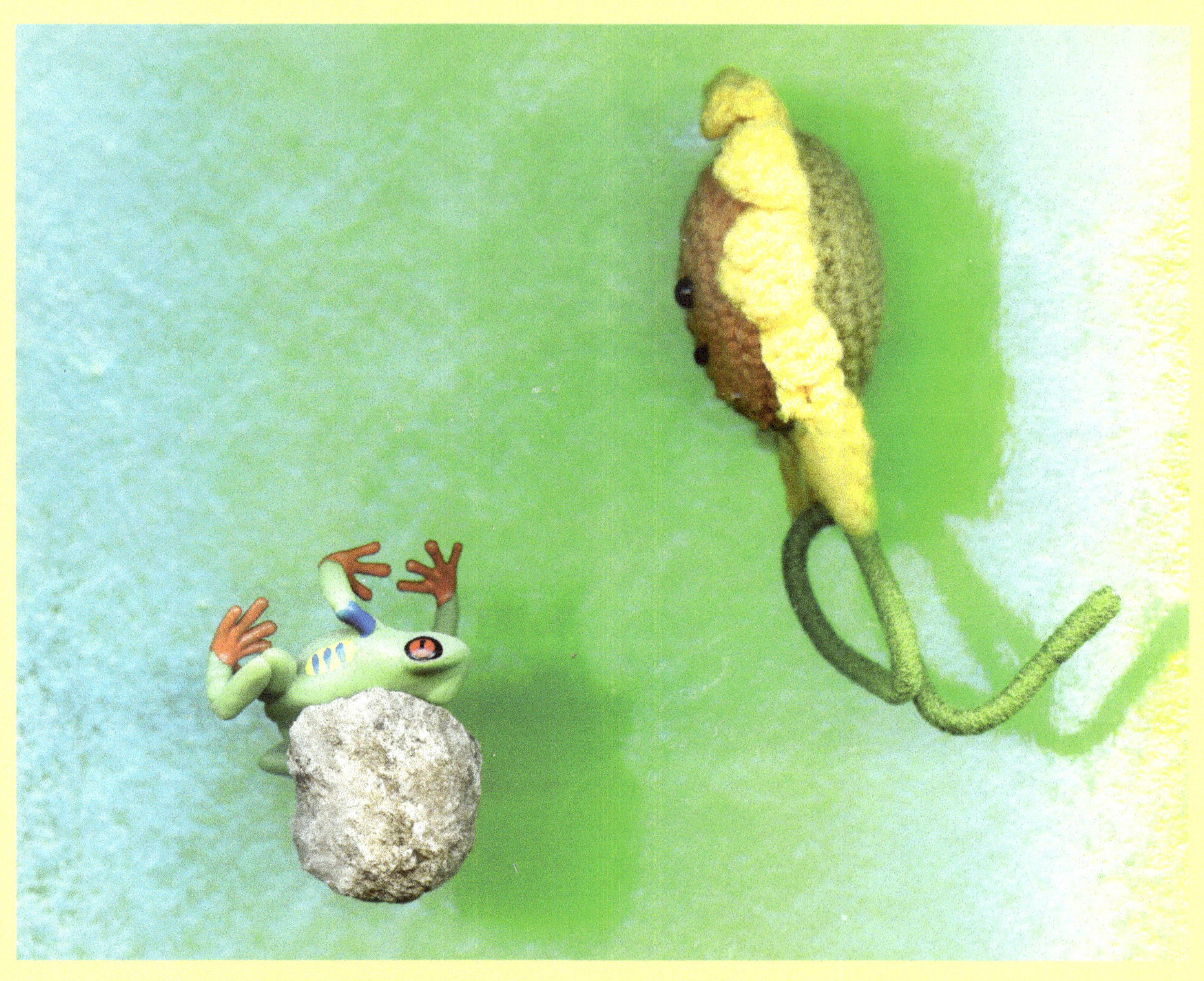

Ginger found Fiona lying on her back on a rock.
Ginger asked Fiona what was wrong.

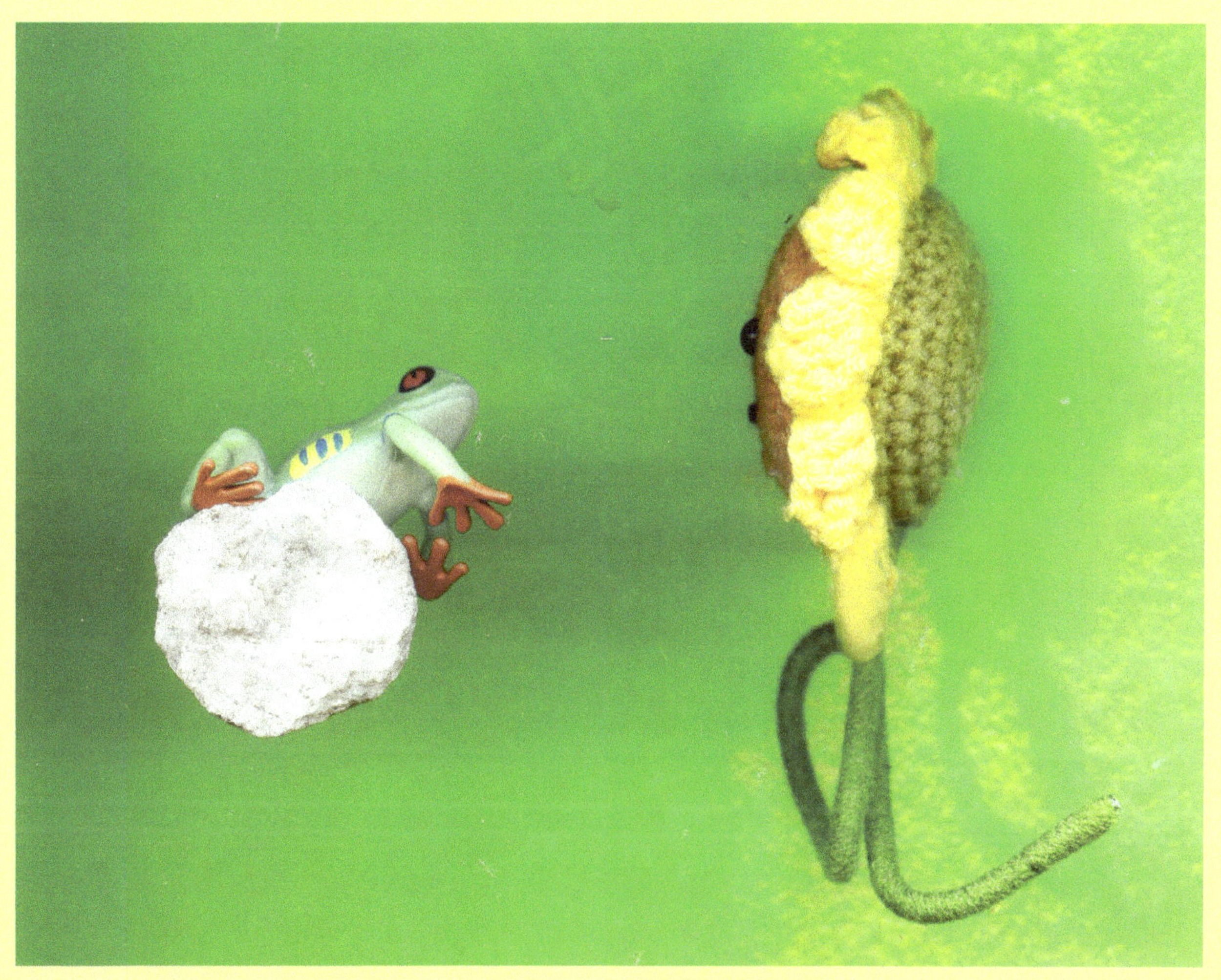

Fiona turned over and told Ginger that her whole family had been eaten by an alligator.

Now she was all alone.

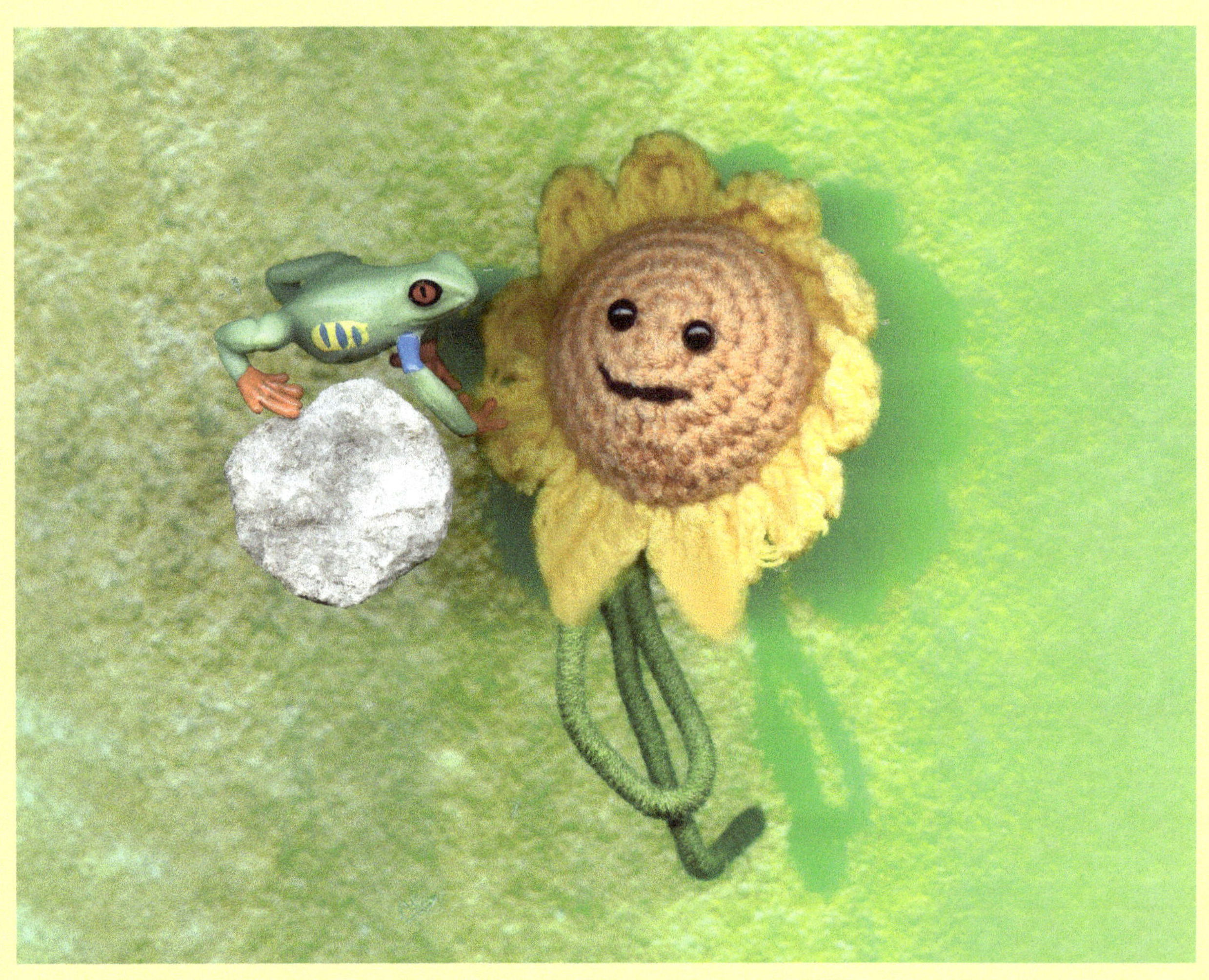

"Not anymore!" said Ginger.

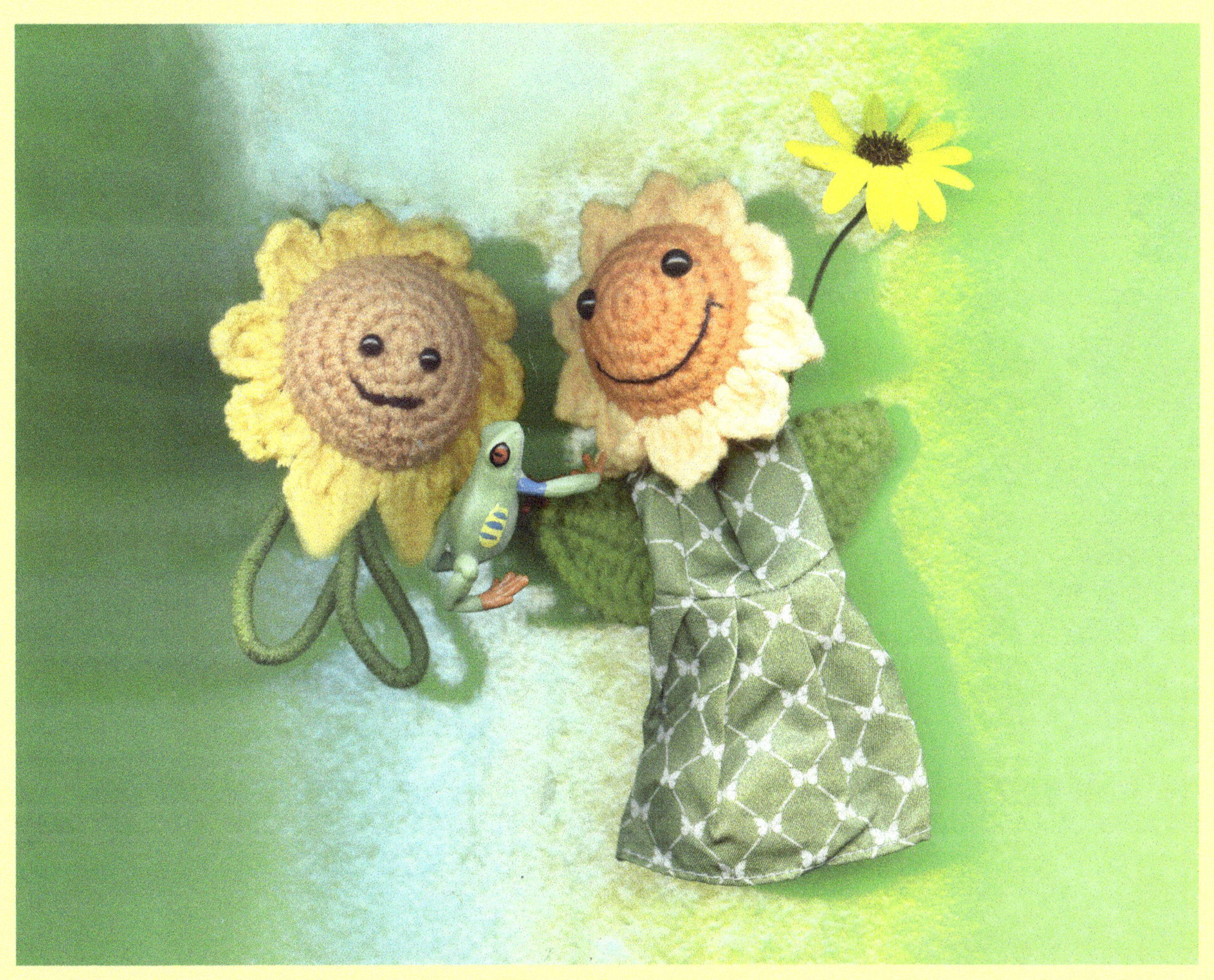

Ginger took Fiona to be with Gramma Bella.

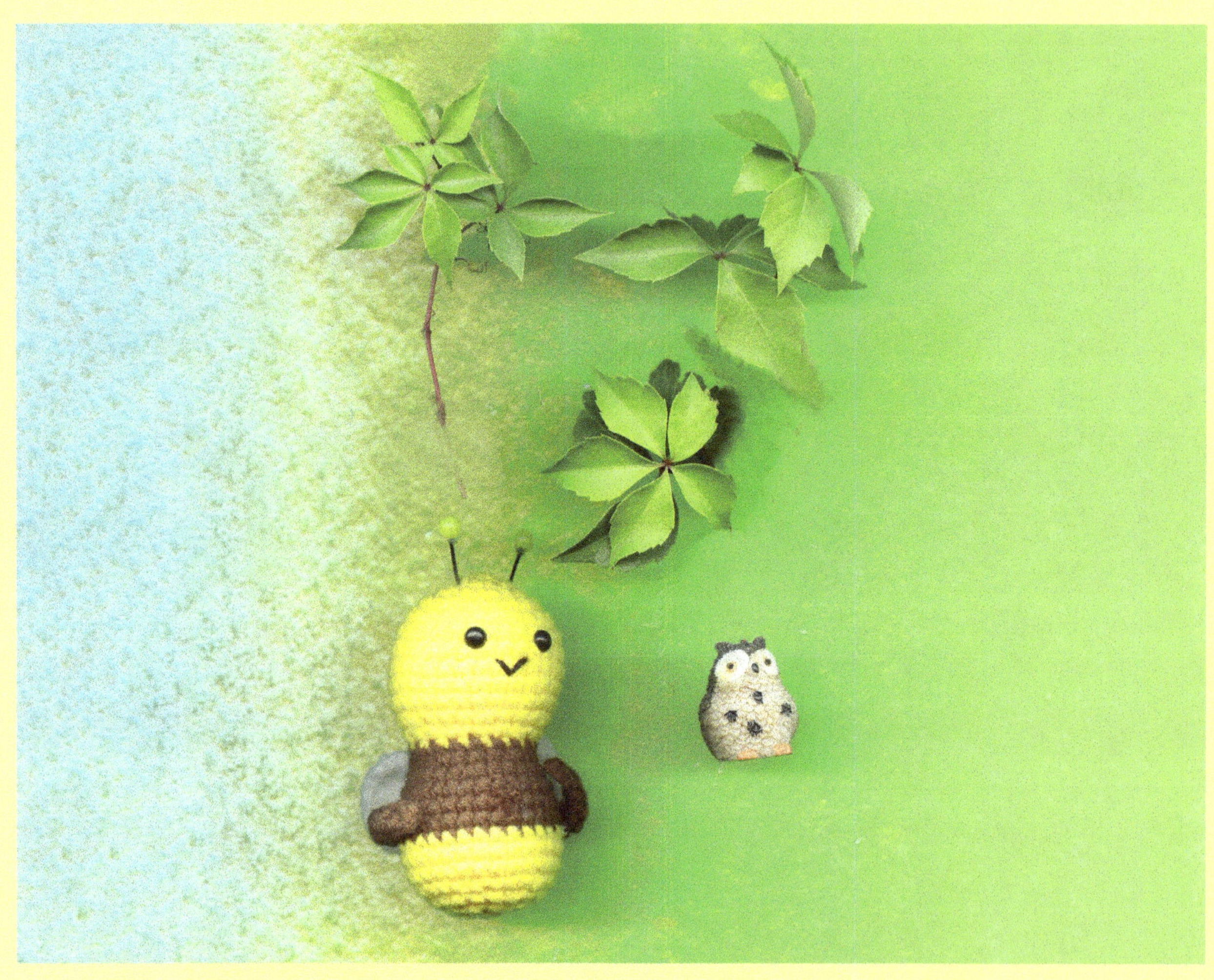

Buzz was out exploring when he found Oscar the Owl with bruises all over his chest.

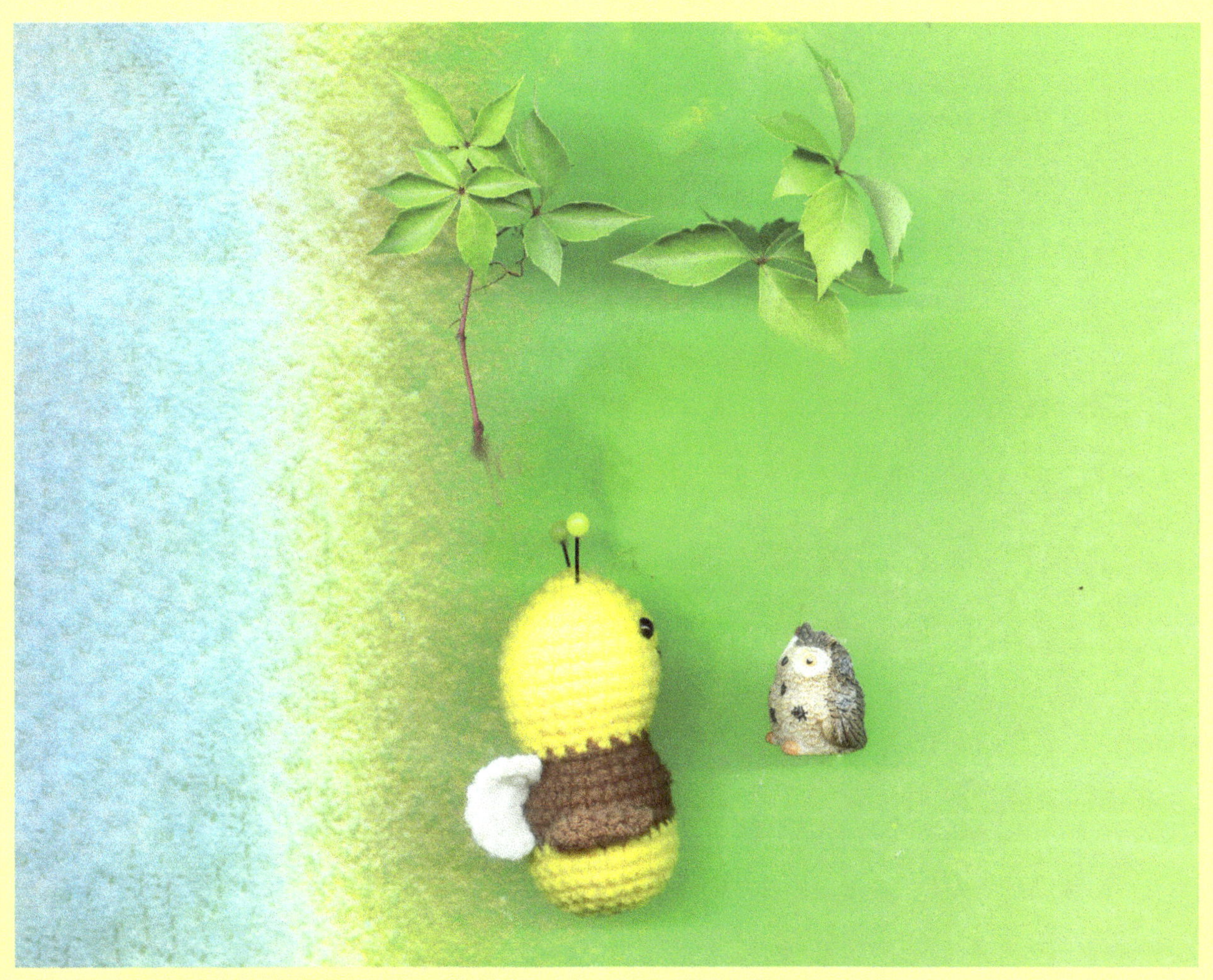

Oscar told Buzz that he had been pecked over
and over again by Bobo the Bully.

He had finally escaped.

But now he was all alone.

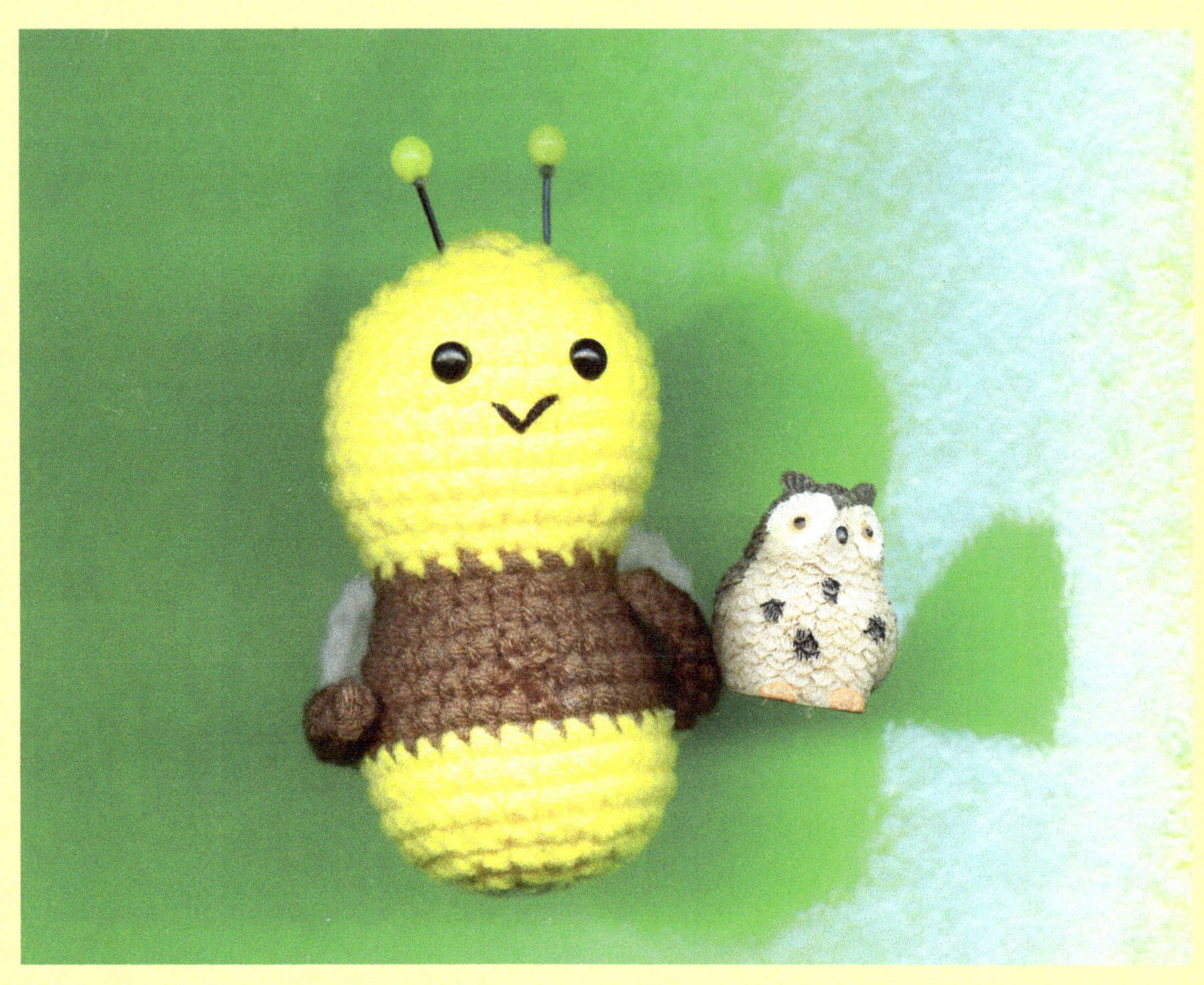

"Not anymore!" said Buzz.

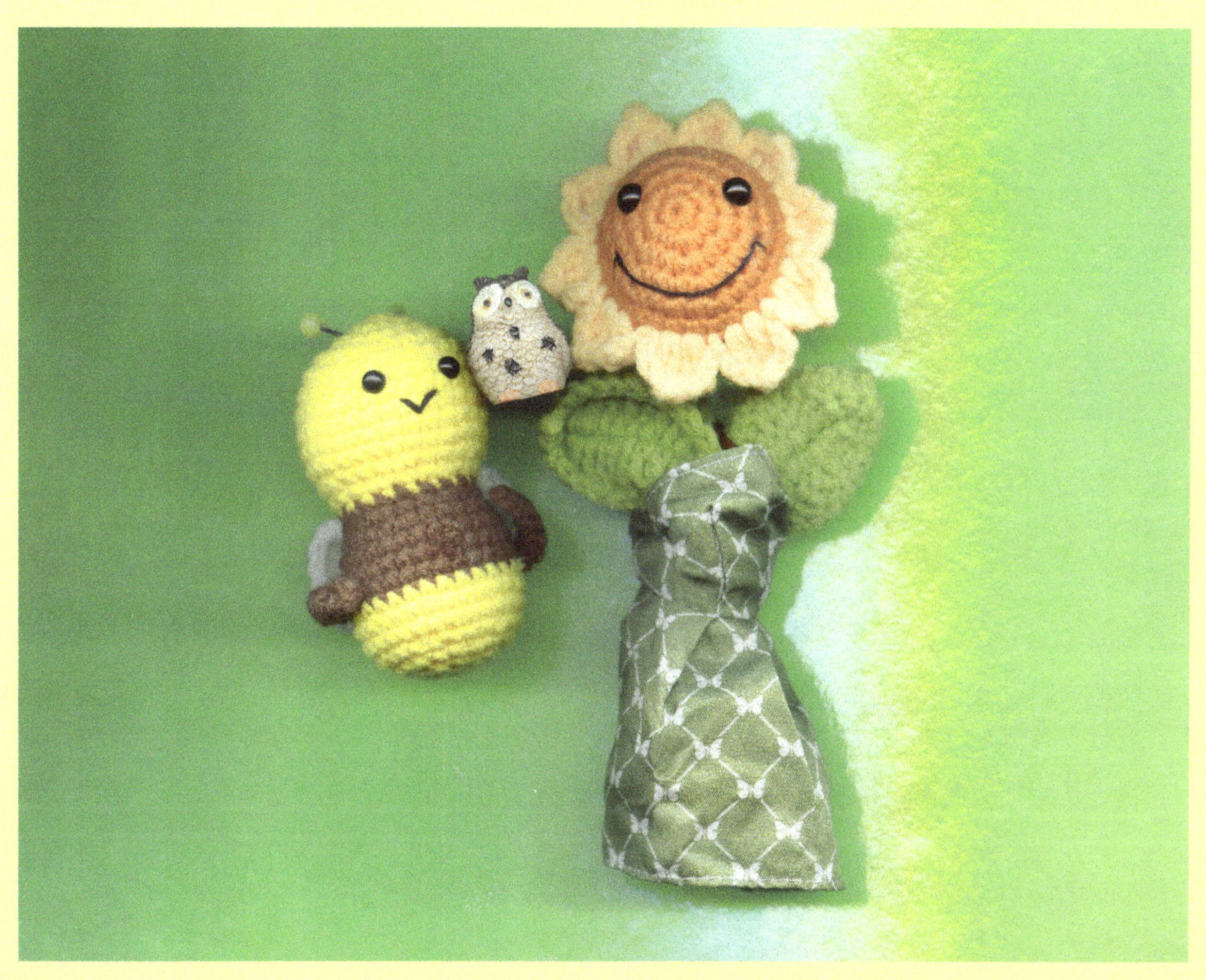

Buzz took Oscar to be with Gramma Bella.
"You will be safe here," Buzz said to Oscar.

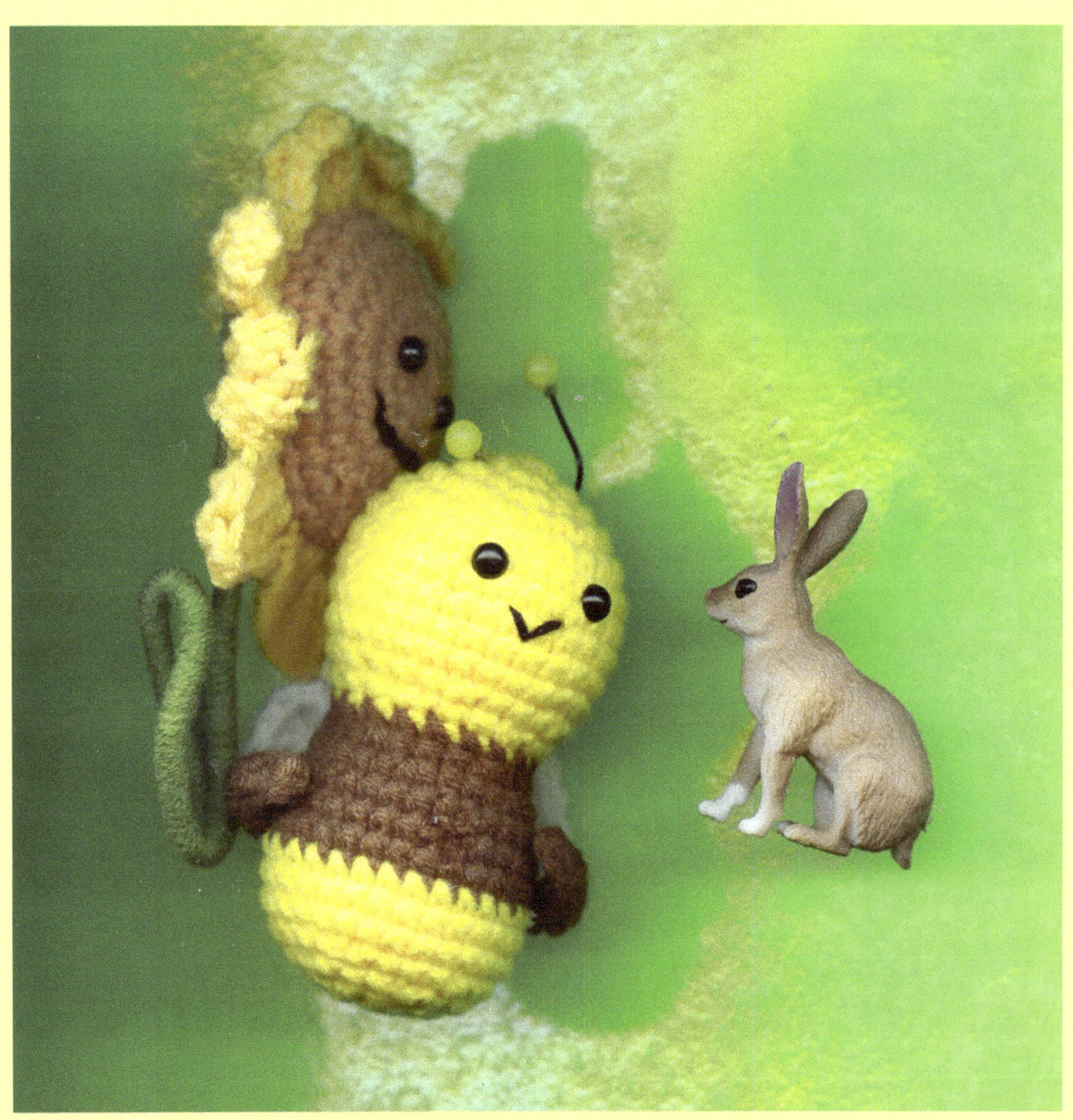

Buzz and Ginger went out together to find their friend Buster Bunny.

They told Buster about the new friends they had found who were now with Gramma Bella.

Buster loved Gramma Bella and said, "It sounds like Gramma could use some help!" "I'll come over soon to meet all your new friends."

Buster became a favorite playmate for Gramma Bella's new family.

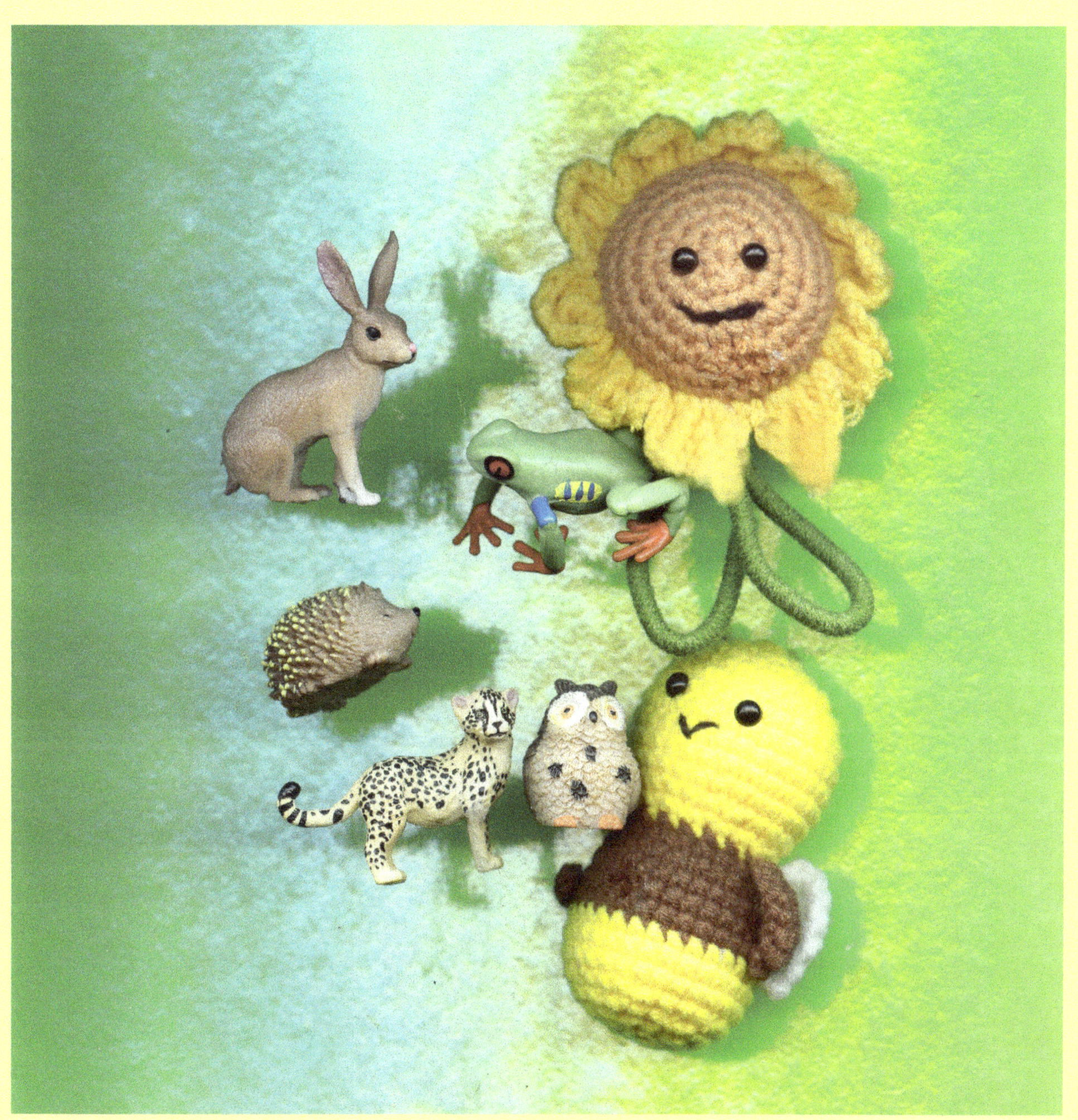

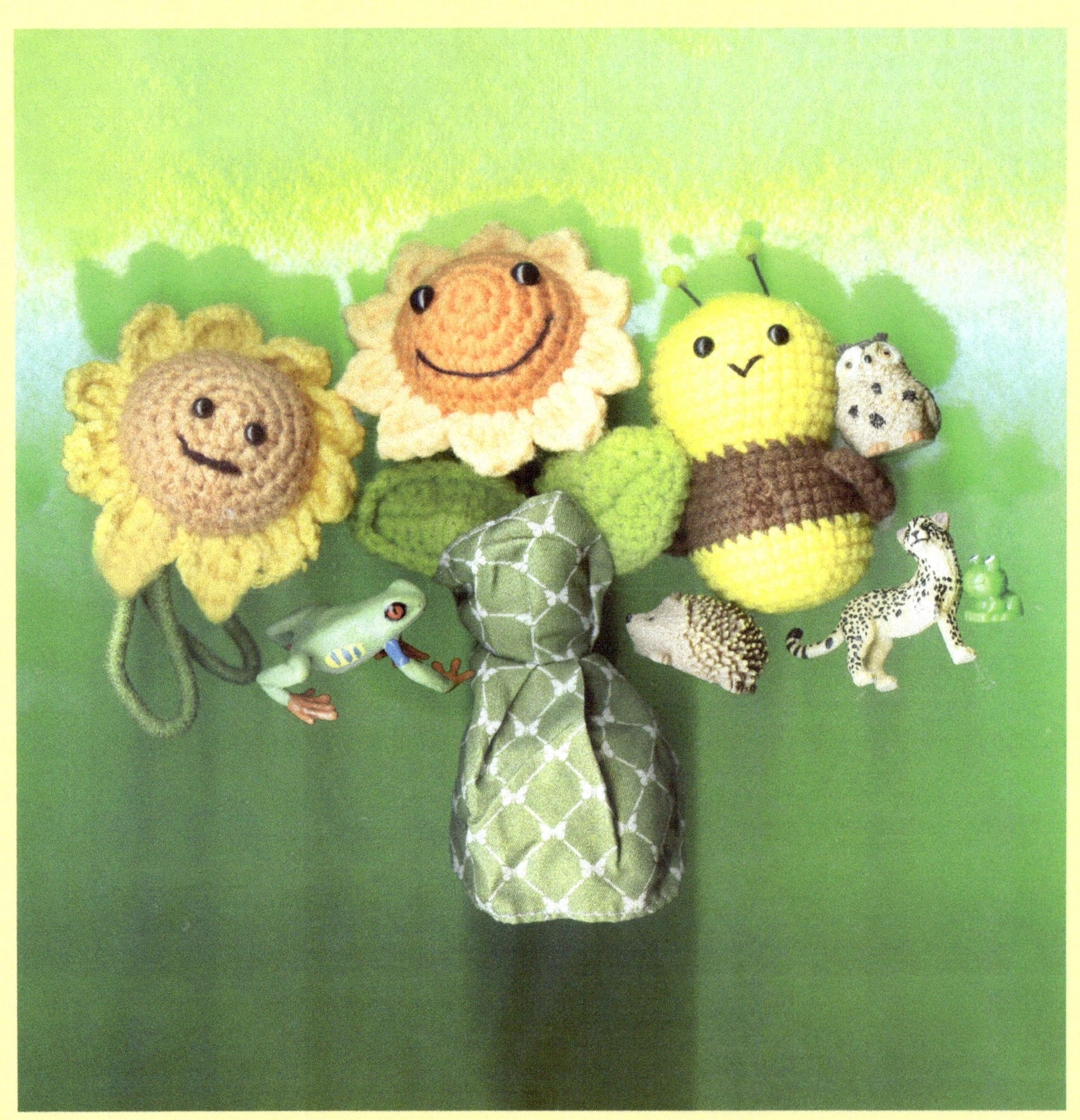

Gramma Bella adopted Harriet, Charley, Fiona and Oscar just as she had adopted Ginger and Buzz.

What a big family she now had!

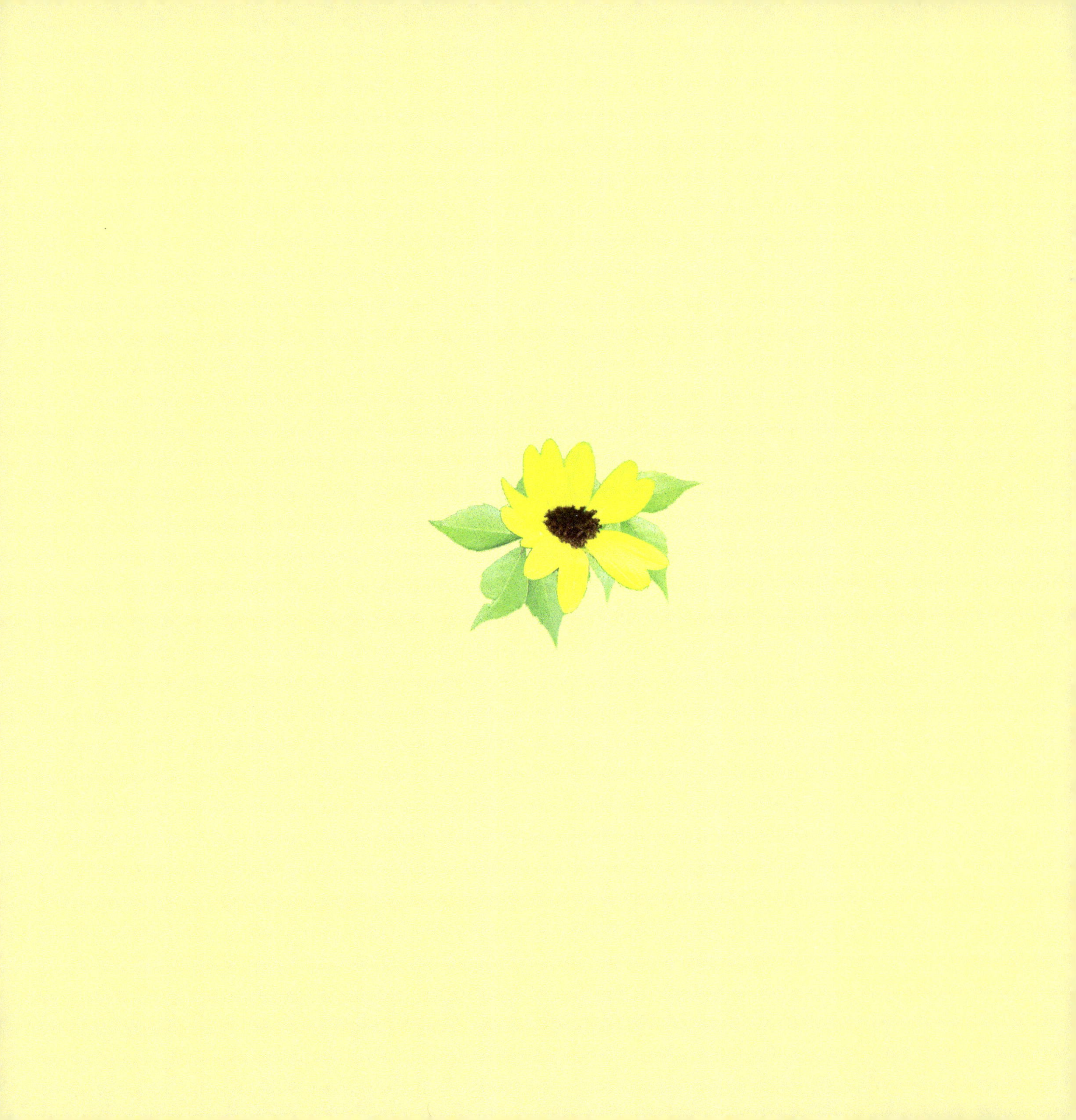

About the Author

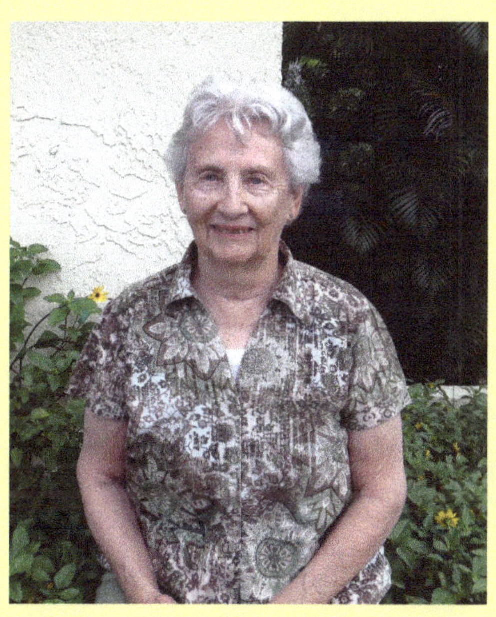

Barbara Guidotti is the author of 17 books in the children's book series, The Wallaboos, two other children's books, *The Kingdom of Treeb* and *It's Not That Nose Upon Your Face*, several inspirational and whimsical gift books filled with original poetry and illustrated with her unique scan-art images, and numerous eBooks.

She has three grown children, three grandchildren, and is former Head Teacher of the Child Study Center at the University of Maine at Orono.

She is now retired and living in Fort Myers, Florida.

Barbara is also an accomplished scan artist. Her work can be seen on her website:

www.naturescanart.com

Also by Barbara Swift Guidotti

Compilations of nature-themed scanned art combined with haiku poetry and quotations to motivate and inspire a celebration of life.

Scanland

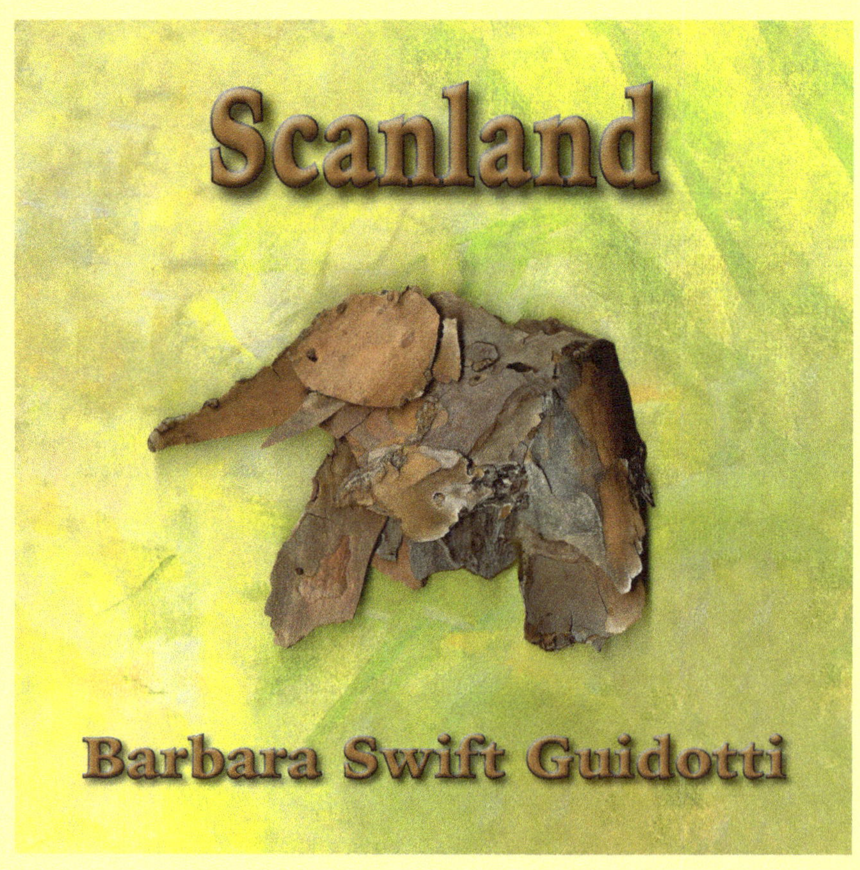

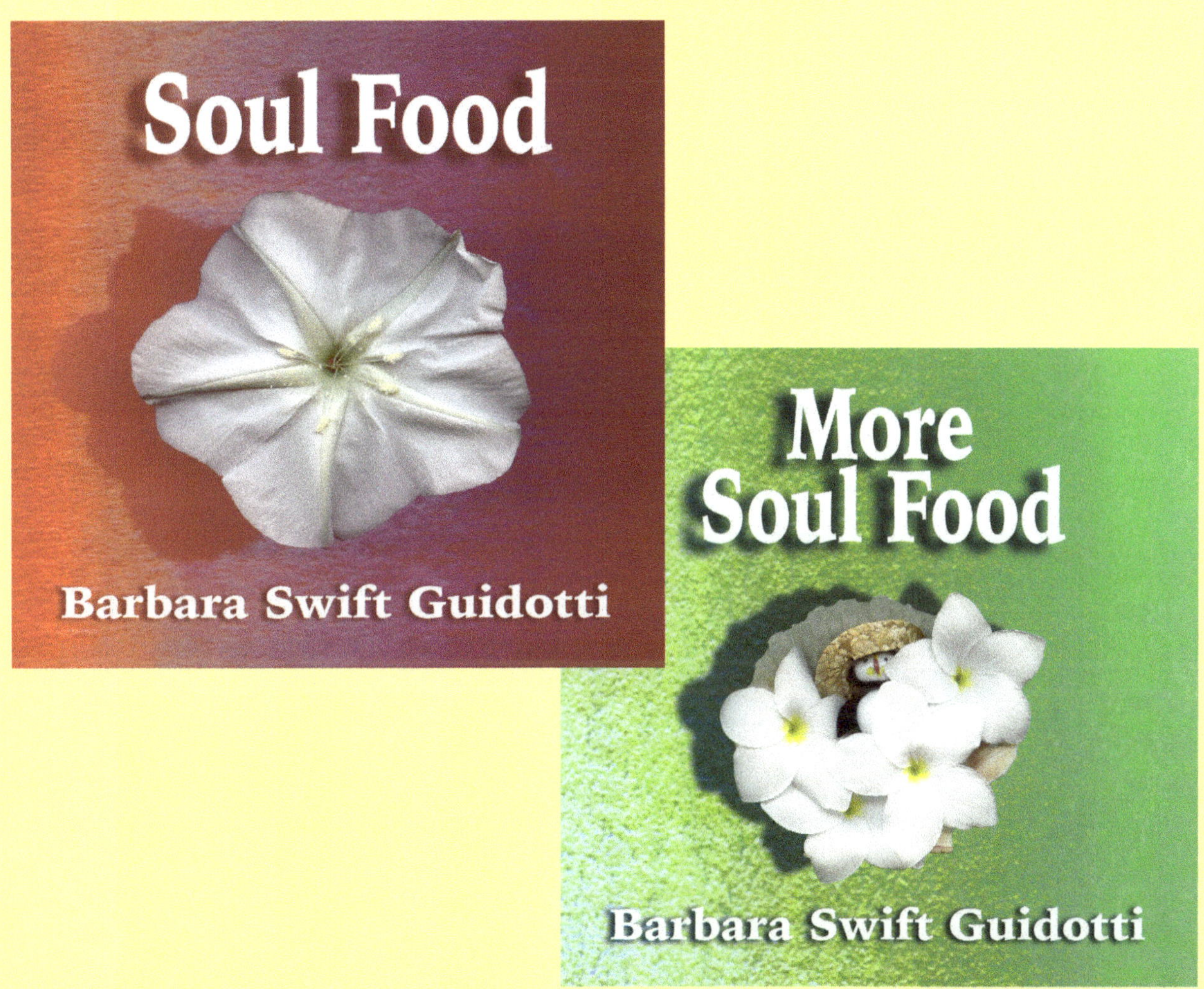
Soul Food
Barbara Swift Guidotti
More
Soul Food
Barbara Swift Guidotti

The Wallaboo Series

It's a wonderful world in Wallaboo Land! The wallaboos will enchant you with their stories and adventures. Imaginary friends, mystical journeys, goofy fun, and delightful, imaginative predicaments await.

The Hiccups Box

The Stardust Trail

The Yellow Echo

The Green Balloon

The Winking Wallaboo Frog

The Bumbleseed Tree

The Giggle Bug

Forget-me-not Land

The Wallaboo Clock

The Wallaboo Treasure

The Baby Wallosaurus

The Humming Bubble

The Wallaboo Songbook

The Wild Wallaboo

Boo-Bear

The Whistling Wallaboo Monster

The Great Ballawoo

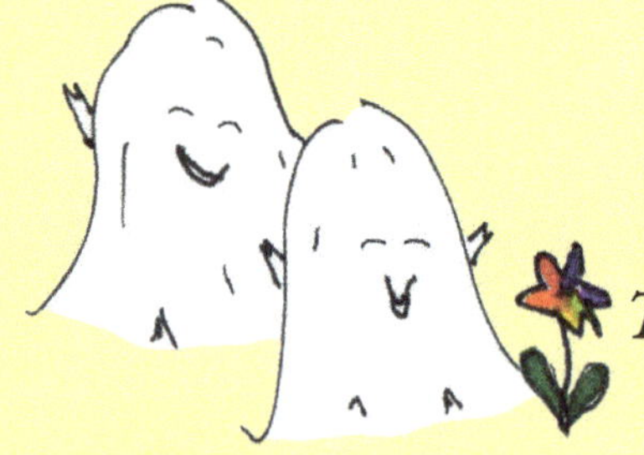

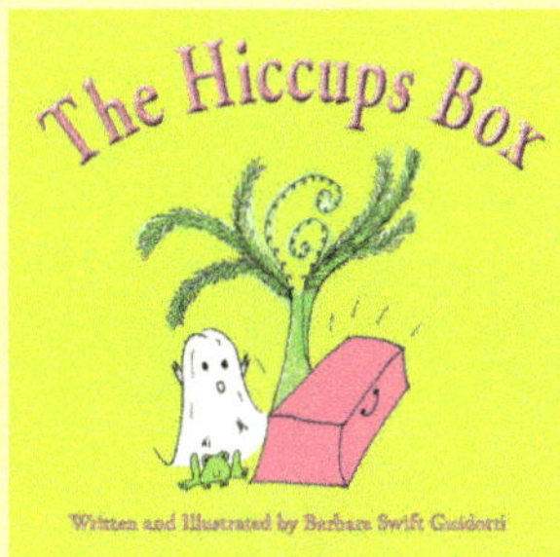

The Hiccups Box
Written and Illustrated by Barbara Swift Guidotti

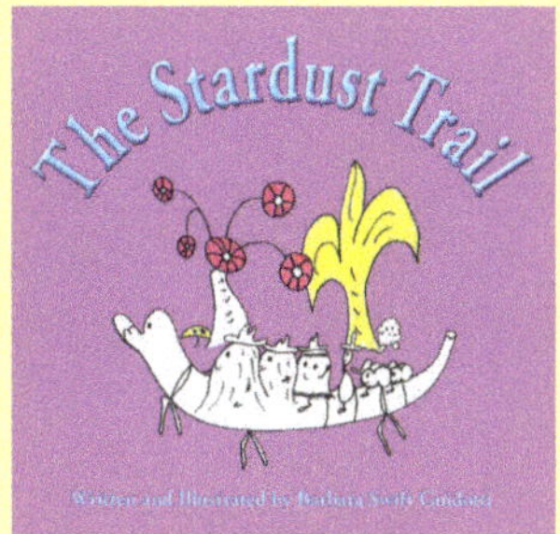

The Stardust Trail
Written and Illustrated by Barbara Swift Guidotti

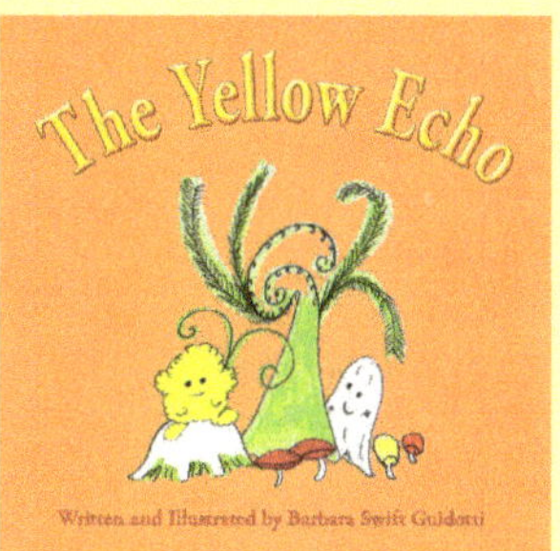

The Yellow Echo
Written and Illustrated by Barbara Swift Guidotti

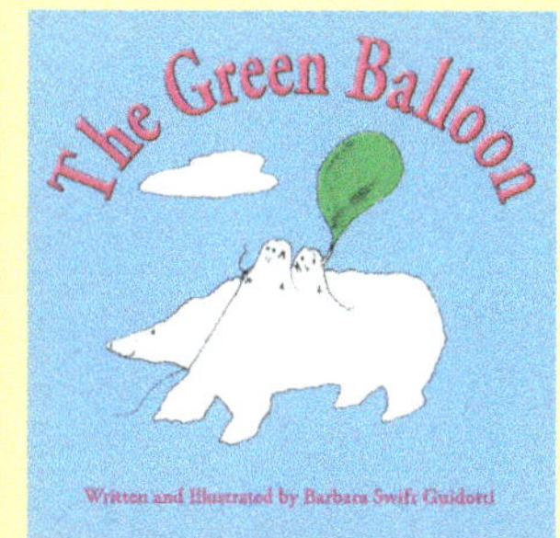

The Green Balloon
Written and Illustrated by Barbara Swift Guidotti

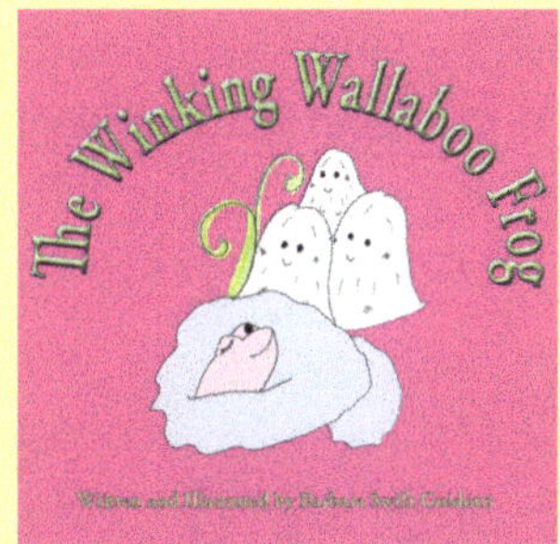

The Winking Wallaboo Frog
Written and Illustrated by Barbara Swift Guidotti

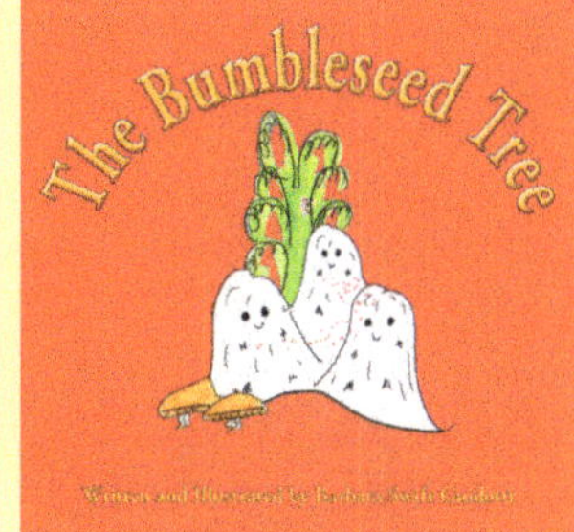

The Bumbleseed Tree
Written and Illustrated by Barbara Swift Guidotti

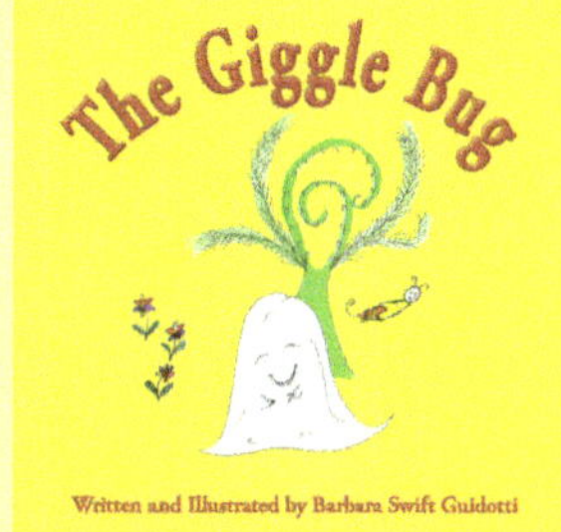

The Giggle Bug
Written and Illustrated by Barbara Swift Guidotti

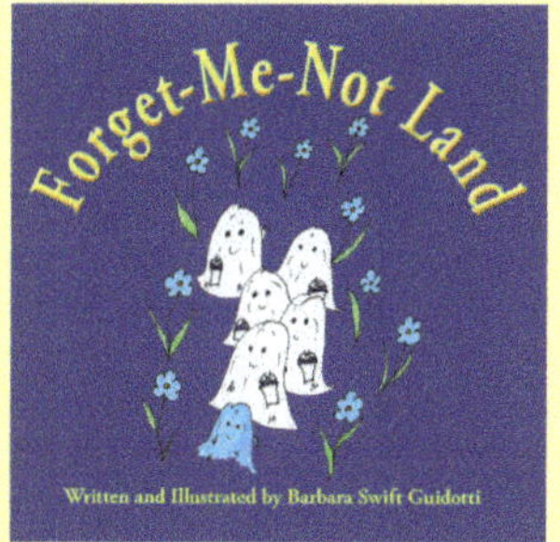

Forget-Me-Not Land
Written and Illustrated by Barbara Swift Guidotti

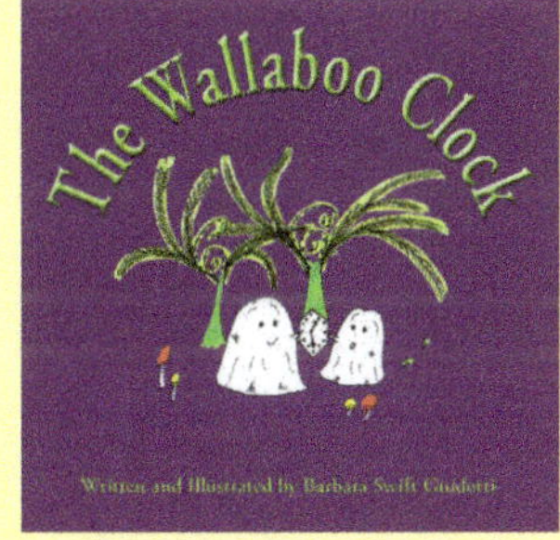

The Wallaboo Clock
Written and Illustrated by Barbara Swift Guidotti

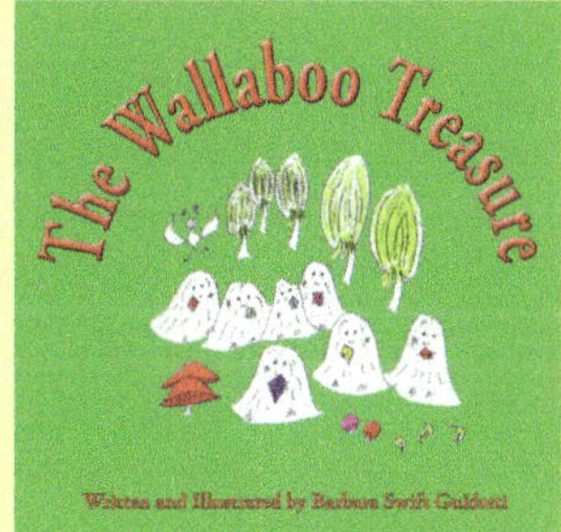

The Wallaboo Treasure
Written and Illustrated by Barbara Swift Guidotti

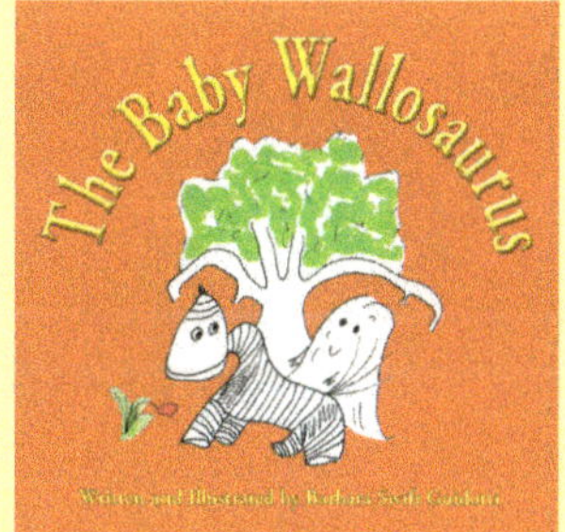

The Baby Wallosaurus
Written and Illustrated by Barbara Swift Guidotti

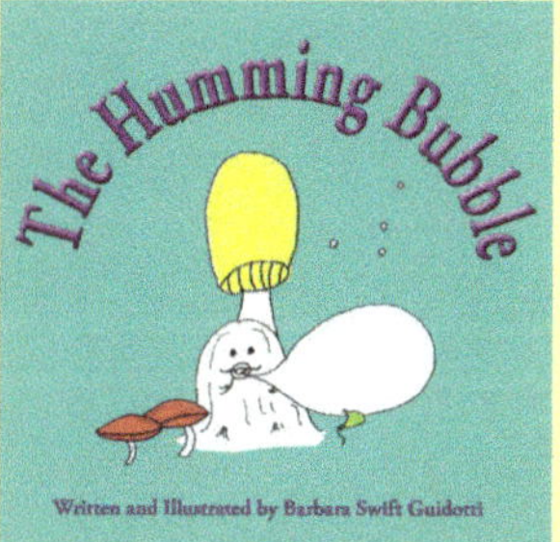

The Humming Bubble
Written and Illustrated by Barbara Swift Guidotti

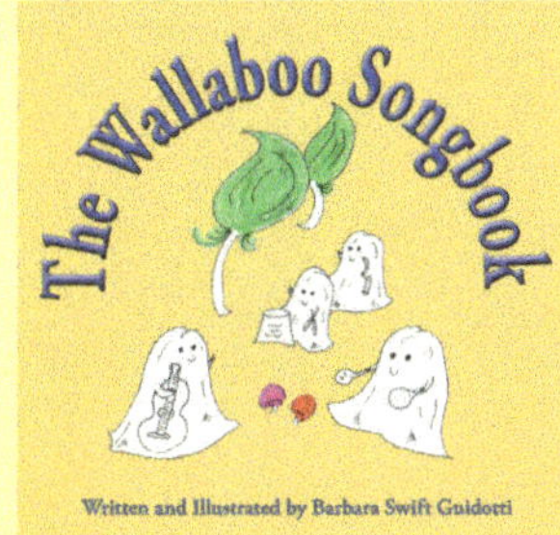

The Wallaboo Songbook
Written and Illustrated by Barbara Swift Guidotti

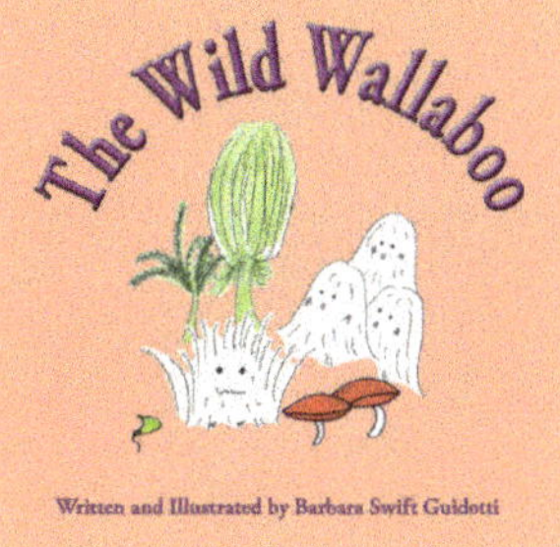

The Wild Wallaboo
Written and Illustrated by Barbara Swift Guidotti

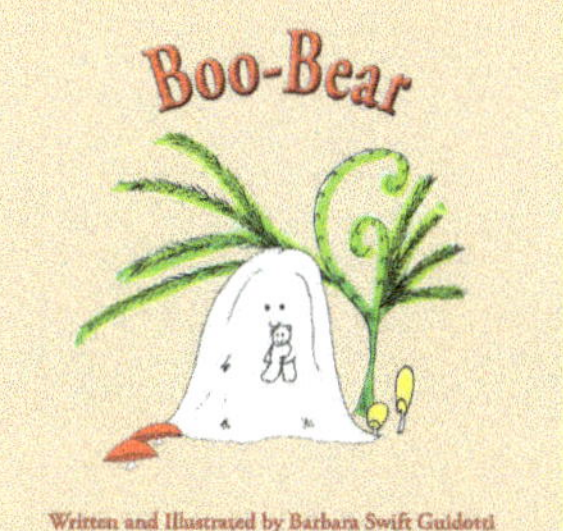

Boo-Bear
Written and Illustrated by Barbara Swift Guidotti

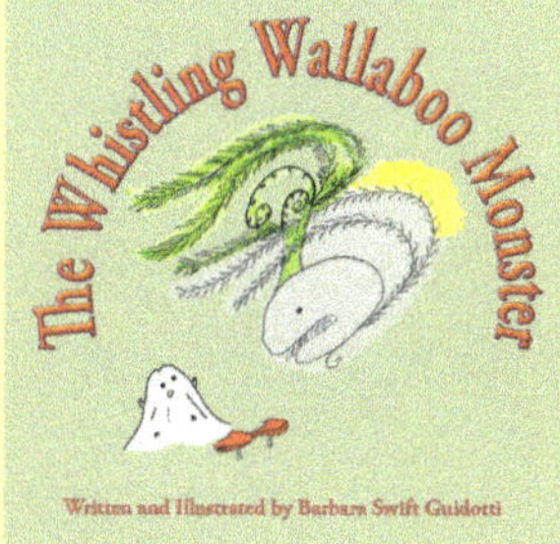

The Whistling Wallaboo Monster
Written and Illustrated by Barbara Swift Guidotti

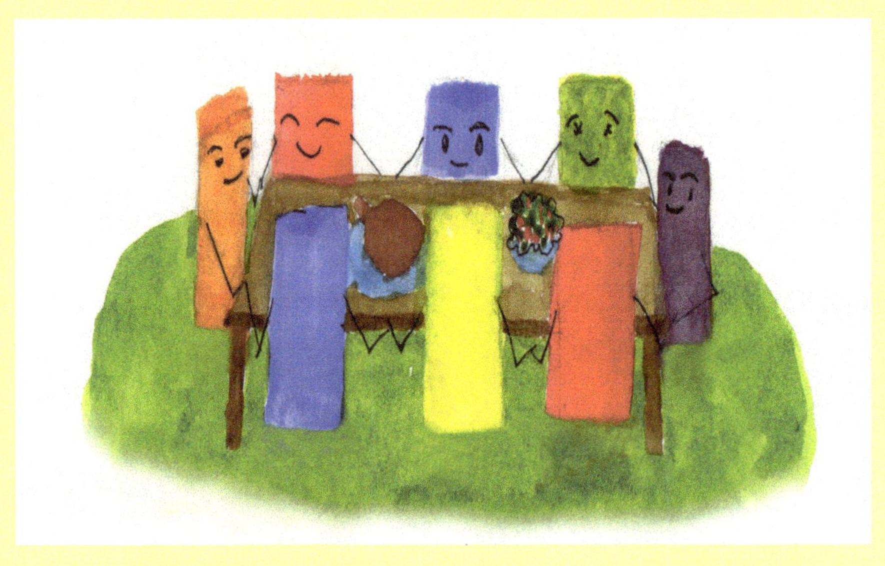

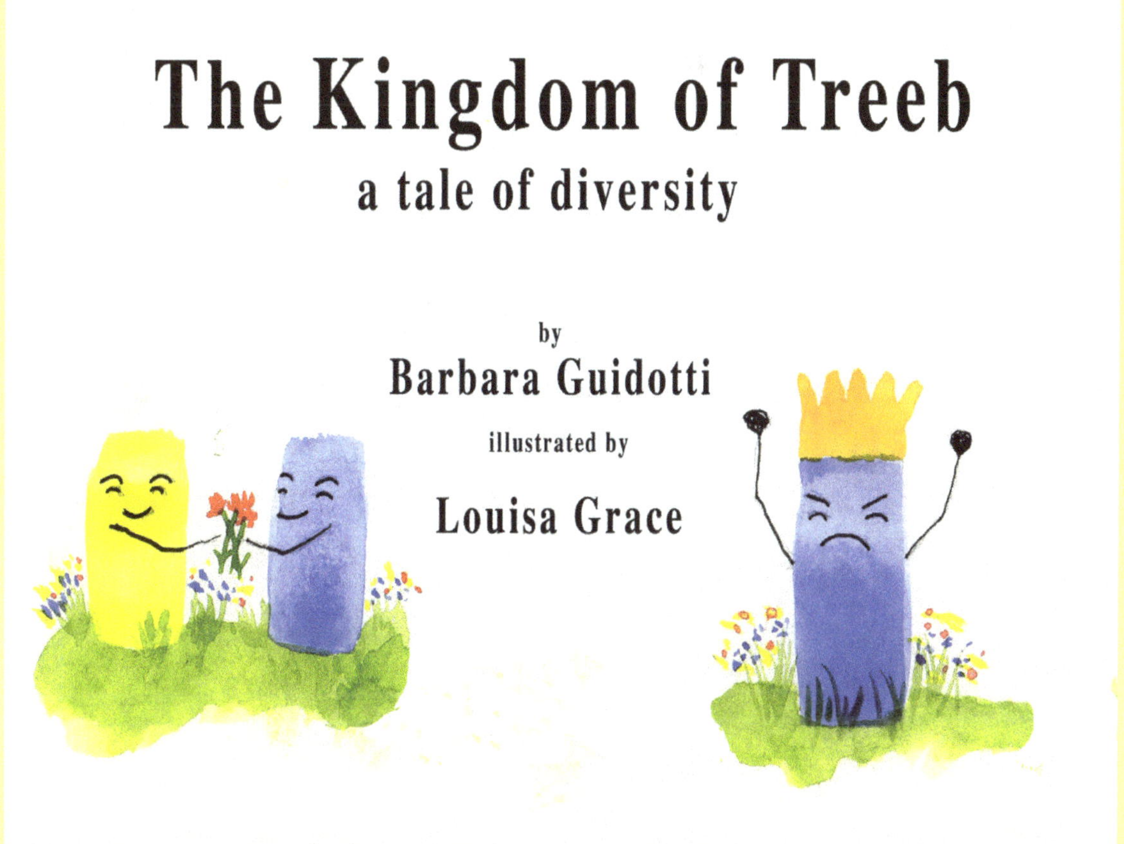

When treebles of a different color come to the Kingdom of Treeb, the king refuses to accept the new arrivals and does his best to keep them and their ways on the other side of the river. Learn how his people enjoy their neighbors in spite of their temperamental leader in this charming and insightful tale of diversity, friendship, and sharing.

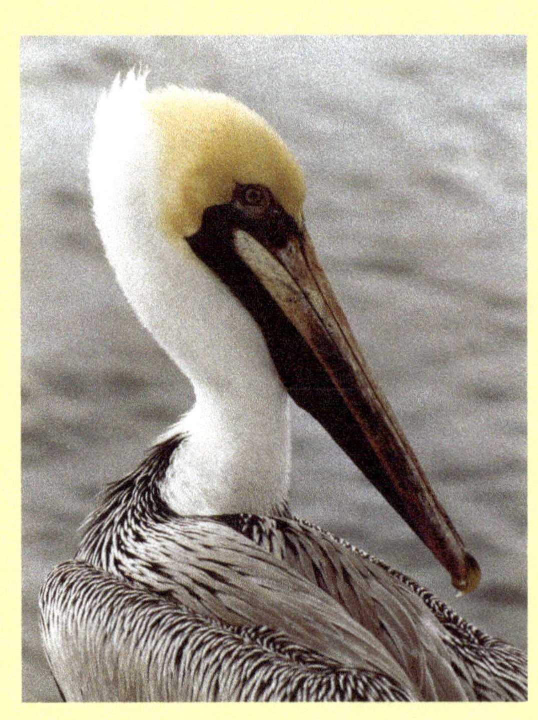

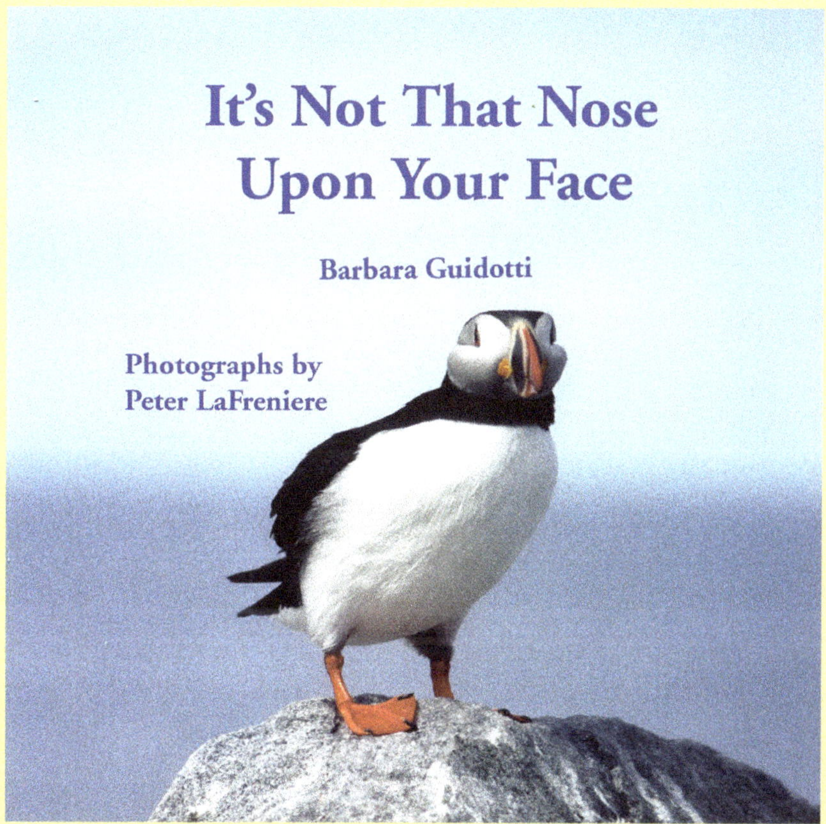

Nature photographs of birds are the inspiration for a book of poetry reflecting views of the world including family, play, and self-image.